Praise for *Soul*

T0032376

"Bill Philipps has become such a pos... somebody who has truly brought me joy, clarity, and, most impor-tantly, peace when I have needed it most. Thrilled he has written *Soul Searching* for all of us to enjoy!"

— **Morgan Stewart McGraw**, television personality

"*Soul Searching* is a beautiful journey into the depths of the human soul. It leads seekers to connect with their inner realm and discover the power to intuitively heal and rise above the many challenges of life."

— **Kim Chestney**, author of
Radical Intuition and founder of IntuitionLab

"Bill Philipps provides a potent, practical blueprint for living a purpose-driven life filled with personal, emotional, and spiritual freedom. This book is a must-have for those who want to let go of the past, embrace the beauty of their life, and feel nourished, peaceful, and supported by the love of Spirit and the incredible power within them."

— **Corin Grillo**, author of *Angel Wealth Magic*

"This book gave me the psychic goosebumps! Bill Philipps shares his deeply touching story of healing and transformation in the pages of this wonderful book. From his own experiences as a young child to his role as a psychic medium, Bill so beautifully presents practical, step-by-step techniques to awaken one's own inner knowing. With each chapter he provides invaluable tools to help you attain your own path to inner peace. A must-read for anyone seeking to transform their life and find the connection with the divine we are all capable of experiencing."

— **MaryAnn DiMarco**, psychic medium and author of
Medium Mentor and *Believe, Ask, Act*

"Bill Philipps has a way of connecting with his readers that goes beyond the powerful stories and meditations in *Soul Searching*. His soul feels present in every paragraph. Bill's authenticity is the real deal."

— **Forbes Robbins Blair**, bestselling author of *Instant Self-Hypnosis*

Praise for *Signs from the Other Side* by Bill Philipps

"Is it truly possible to receive communications from beyond? Bill Philipps's book is an unpretentious exploration into afterlife communication and offers illustrations and tools that tell readers that yes, indeed, it is. The book is a pleasure to read and will bring comfort to those who read it. I recommend that anyone interested in this topic read *Signs from the Other Side*."

— **Raymond Moody, MD, PhD**, author of *Life After Life*

"For many, a spiritual awakening first occurs when they hear a message from a loved one who has passed to the other side. It becomes an all-important doorway to contacting the universal energy we are surrounded by on a daily basis but have not been trained to see or connect with. In this book, Bill Philipps lovingly brings you, the reader, his gift of helping others make this connection. The stories and lessons in *Signs from the Other Side* remind us that there is more to life, and our relationships, than meets the eye. And when we open to that, magic starts to happen."

— **Lee Harris**, author of *Energy Speaks*

SOUL
SEARCHING

SOUL
SEARCHING

*Tune In to Spirit and Awaken
Your Inner Wisdom*

BILL PHILIPPS
with William Croyle

New World Library
Novato, California

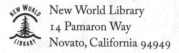

New World Library
14 Pamaron Way
Novato, California 94949

Text design by Tona Pearce Myers

Library of Congress Cataloging-in-Publication data is available.

First printing, April 2023
ISBN 978-1-60868-814-2
Ebook ISBN 978-1-60868-815-9

Printed in Canada on 100% postconsumer-waste recycled paper

New World Library is proud to be a Gold Certified Environmentally Responsible Publisher. Publisher certification awarded by Green Press Initiative.

10   9   8   7   6   5   4   3   2   1

*I dedicate this book to all those who yearn for a deeper way
to connect with the invisible world, to gain new paths
of access to the realm of Spirit; and those who share
with me a lifelong desire to journey in search
of our personal doorway to the soul.*

CONTENTS

INTRODUCTION

We are born into this world as virtuous spiritual beings, yet we are vulnerable to our experiences and environments. As we age, we are indoctrinated with a belief system that gradually turns us into imperfect humans. But no matter who we become, that innocence at birth — the purest version of ourselves — is eternally part of our fabric. Those gifts we entered this life with, no matter how out of reach they may appear, are always accessible.

To tap into them requires our conscious self to acknowledge our subconscious self. In other words, we need the earthly person we are now to open the door to that spiritual side — that imaginative, honest, and loving child who is ready to listen to and guide us.

Connecting with our higher self helps us navigate and flourish in a world that is becoming increasingly complex. Such a connection takes significant work and a lot of soul searching, but we have the power to make it through conscious choice. It is up to us.

I know intuitively, psychically, and as a medium that there is a powerful energy on the smallest of scales pervasive throughout the Universe — where our greatest potential lies waiting to come to fruition. This is where Spirit's influence resides, in the thin veil between our two realms. I believe it is our free will that determines whether we choose to sense that energy, to give it credence, so we may create our own version of heaven on earth.

Chapter 1

THE CHILD WITHIN

The cry we hear from deep in our hearts comes from the wounded child within. Healing this inner child's pain is the key to transforming anger, sadness, and fear.

— THICH NHAT HANH

When I was in second grade and living in Brooklyn, New York, our elementary school's fundraiser was for each student to sell wrapping paper. While many of my classmates sold theirs to parents and relatives, I didn't have that luxury. My dad was in California. My mom, impoverished and struggling to survive day to day, was my primary caretaker yet rarely around. She and I relied on food banks for nourishment and on the kindness of people we barely knew to house us off and on during my time in Brooklyn. The only way I could sell was to go out alone, door to door.

I canvased the neighborhood after school and on weekends for about two weeks, carefully placing the money I collected each day in my top dresser drawer for safekeeping.

The morning after I finally hit my personal goal of forty dollars, I got dressed and reached into the drawer to bring the money to school, but it was gone — every dollar. I panicked as I dug deep into my pockets, searched under my bed, and rustled through my backpack, but it was futile. All of it had been in that drawer when I went to sleep. Without it, I couldn't deliver the wrapping paper to the people who bought it, nor could I refund them. I was scared, but maybe even more so, heartbroken — because I knew who had taken it.

My mom sometimes "borrowed" money from me to pay her debts or get her next hit. And when the money disappeared, so did she, often for days at a time. I always knew she would come home, and sometimes she eventually paid me back. Either way, I never questioned her, for I was too respectful and loved her too much — she was still my mom, after all. This time was different. The money wasn't mine, and I had to say something.

"Mom," I said when she returned home four days later. "My money from the wrapping paper sales is missing."

To this day, I recall seeing my mom standing in the doorway to my bedroom, looking worn and tired as she stared at me with a blank look. Her reply was a punch in the gut.

"Well, did you lose it somewhere?"

"Um, no. It was all in my top drawer."

"Well," she said, "I don't know what to tell you." Then she turned and walked out of the room.

I knew in my heart she was lying, and I was devastated.

A couple of days later, sober and feeling guilty, my mom came clean about her actions. She told me that she had indeed taken the cash to pay bills, but she promised to pay me back in a day or two. I believed her, but she never did.

Desperate, I told the people we were staying with, the Fosters, what happened. I was consumed with fear, embarrassment, and shame for having to ask them for help. I felt alone at that moment. Thankfully, they were sympathetic enough to give me the forty dollars to replace what my mom had taken.

We all have the gift of hindsight that we can use to navigate the road ahead, which leads to the question: What do we wish we knew as children that we know now that could have helped us then? More than anything, I wish I knew then that fear is a choice and that we can shift our thoughts and actions from negative to positive. This concept can be difficult even for an adult to grasp. Still, the possibility and power are always there, and the younger we learn how to do it, the sooner we can direct the trajectory of our lives toward a destiny of happiness and fulfillment.

When I was a kid, the adults around me were untrustworthy, to put it kindly, and my fear abounded. Fear of where I would live each day. Fear of going to bed hungry. Fear of being alone. Fear of having nobody to turn to if I needed help with anything. Fear of just being with my parents.

About a year or so before the wrapping-paper incident, when I was six years old, I was living with both my parents in Southern California. My dad was using drugs and often abused my mom, which I witnessed. My mom used drugs and alcohol as well, and she also had a boyfriend on the side. I feel she became involved with this other man because of her addictions and a deep-seated need to be taken care of. After a while, my mom wanted out of the toxic relationship with my dad, so one day she ran away when Dad wasn't home and took me with her. We spent that first night in an abandoned school bus in a ditch lit by lanterns. There were eight other people there using heroin and performing sex acts on one another. I pushed my way to a seat in the back, covered my ears, and closed my eyes to escape this horrible scene. Mom kissed me on the forehead and told me she loved me, and then she joined her friends.

In retrospect, as awful as that experience was, it was probably one of the first times that I learned how to deal with fear, at least to the extent that a six-year-old can in that kind of situation. Closing my eyes and ears to the earthly world gave me some internal comfort because I could use my mind to shield myself from the pain around me. This miraculous experience was the first time I saw the healing white light, which profoundly changed me. While I was in the physical presence of monstrous acts being committed, I was shielded from them by shutting out the outside world and going within. As I grew up and reflected on that night in the bus, I realized it was in that difficult moment when I first surrendered to something greater than me. That's *why* I saw the white light — my higher power. I have since embraced my connection to the spirit world by continuously seeking this white light of protection, which is now one of my daily practices.

Closing my eyes and ears and going within myself allows me to redirect my thoughts. I first focus on my breath, which brings a sense of calm and renews my life source. As I focus on my breath and keep that continuous motion flowing, I have the power to access a part of me, an "added space" within, that allows me to choose where I want to direct my energy. I believe in the philosophy that we all have free will and can pick the path we take, but often we feel like we have no choices and are prisoners in our minds. It's truly magical what can happen, though, when we pause, focus on our breath, and enter that other world. This meditative state, known in Eastern religions as Nirvana, is the bridge between our physical world and the realm of Spirit.

Later, my paternal grandmother provided me with the religious foundation that contributed to my epiphany about what I had experienced on the bus, and for that, I am eternally grateful. When I was nine, my mom was in no condition to take care of me anymore, and so I returned to California to live with my grandma and my dad. Grandma was heavy into the Bible. I went to church with her occasionally and watched biblical cartoons on television. Today, our belief systems travel along different paths, but there are many commonalities — namely, our faith in someone or something greater than ourselves and the importance of surrendering to that higher power. Having that belief system instilled in me gave me an inner peace as a child that said, "Billy, you're going to be okay." I didn't necessarily know how or why; I just knew that I was protected. Today, I know that protection comes from Spirit, which I can access and feel anytime I use my spiritual tools, such as meditation and intention-setting. I discuss the practice of setting intentions in chapter 11, but it all starts with meditation.

Meditation doesn't necessarily mean sitting in the traditional lotus pose with one's legs crossed. It could mean what I experienced in the back of that abandoned bus: being curled up in a ball, my eyes shut and hands over my ears, as I thought about the things and places that made me happy, which pulled me out of chaos. As an adult, I explain meditation as a positive practice that disconnects us from the rational part of our being and minds. I do that today with a vigorous workout every morning, which helps me dump heavy and useless energy, find clarity, and ground myself.

Intention-setting is just as it sounds: stating our intention for what we want to experience. I think of an intention as getting the ball rolling toward something that amasses enough strength and energy that it cannot be denied. It's not something that can be put on autopilot, thus the word *intention*. It is how we approach our day, a person, or a specific situation. It's setting a positive tone toward how we will live right now and in the moments to come.

Having such access to Spirit means having intuition and trusting what I'm feeling. How often have you felt something in your gut, only to be told or even mocked by others that you're wrong or paranoid? Then you begin to doubt yourself, even though your gut continues to insist otherwise. That is your intuition — Spirit trying to communicate with you. It may take time, but the truth will eventually emerge if you trust what you feel. As children, we sense our intuitions, only to have adults doubt us. Because they are adults, the people we look to for guidance, we ultimately follow them instead.

If I could, I would tell the child version of me to not be afraid, to trust what I feel, and to be aware that a support system exists on the other side that can be called upon for comfort. That support system is whatever we believe it to be, depending on our faith or upbringing. We might call it God the Father, Jesus Christ, the Holy Spirit, Ganesh, Shiva, or even the Universe, the stars, or an indescribable energy. And I would nurture that child with so much love that he knew he was not alone. The traumas from my childhood made it difficult to trust myself because I wasn't getting reassurance from the adults closest to me. But over time, as my grandmother taught me about the power of prayer and about the healing that comes from faith in a divine source, I learned to accept what I felt as real.

The force field that I felt protecting me on that bus was legit, and I have carried this understanding with me ever since, especially in my most difficult times. Now I know that force field is the light of Spirit, the light of God, and we all have access to it — not just as adults, but as children. The sooner we recognize and acknowledge it, the happier and more meaningful our lives will be.

Engaging with the light of Spirit, an all-powerful and loving force, is something I do as part of my daily spiritual practice. It's become so ingrained in me that I don't always think consciously about it when I do it. Because these practices have changed me in such positive ways, I want to share these tools with you. At the end of chapters 1 through 14, I have provided a "daily practice." These are meditations, prayers, and guided visualizations that you can do yourself. They're designed to progress through the book and to embody the concepts in each chapter. You may find yourself drawn more toward one or another, but I encourage you to try each practice at least once. Later, you can return again to the practices you prefer. My aim is to provide you with a toolbox of techniques to refer to whenever you need them.

DAILY PRACTICE

Healing the Child Within

In this meditation, you meet and engage with your inner child. Facing your inner child is the first step in your personal transformation. Through the use of positive and nurturing reinforcement, who you were as a child and who you are now become whole again.

Focus solely on your breath. Breathe in slowly and hold it for a second, feeling the expanse of your belly and rib cage. Now slowly exhale and send out with your breath everything that is on your mind — the to-do lists, all future needs, worries of the past, all the unsettled energy of the day. Continue to do this as many times as you need until you feel cleansed, relaxed, and in a peaceful space. This is the space you need to be in to embrace your higher self and bring about positive change. Use your breath to achieve this before every daily practice.

Now, visualize a door you walked through as a child, a door to a safe place — maybe your childhood bedroom. If you visualize a door that does not feel right or safe to walk through, visualize a different door until you find one that does feel safe. Maybe the door to your grandmother's home, a clubhouse in your backyard, or your best friend's house.

As you open the door, see your child self in the room. They are sitting, head down, on a bed, bench, or couch, depending on where you are. Walk up to this child and extend your hand to offer support. See the child look up at you with hope in their eyes. With a heart full of trust, they gently take your hand. Lock eyes with them and tell them how much they are loved, gifted, brave, and capable. Tell them that the sky is the limit; they can achieve and overcome anything. They are always supported and cherished, even when they don't see or feel it. Notice the child smiling, lighting up with excitement, as they eagerly stand and hug you with all their love and might. In this moment of connection, tell them that you're always there for them. Always. All they need to do is meet you back in this room, which is now filled with a dazzling white light. As you focus on this scene, your energy blends with this child. The two of you are one. You always have been one, and you always will be.

From this moment forward, know that you are limitless, loved, and supported in all your endeavors. Before you leave, look back at the child, who is beaming with love and confidence. Feel this energy in your heart as you exit the room, and take it wherever you go.

This feeling of support at such a young age is crucial to trusting yourself and those around you. It allows you to live your life with greater peace and to achieve what you want most. It permits you to have an open and empathetic heart. When we know that we're always supported — in all ways and at all times — our fear diminishes, and we can move forward with confidence and clarity. This is how our true gifts shine.

Working with your inner child in this way can help remove any negative programming you brought with you into adulthood. Clearing the subconscious mind allows you to feel excited about sharing your most authentic self with the world. As with any habit, repetition is the key to breaking bad habits and, at the same time, forming new, better habits. Try to do this often, daily if you can, and even more frequently during periods of doubt.

Chapter 2

LETTING GO

Accept what is, let go of what was, and have faith in what will be.

— SONIA RICOTTI

A key to living the life we desire is to let go of what doesn't serve us to make room for everything that does. This means letting go of three elements that infiltrate our lives:

- Past transgressions (ours and those of others)
- Toxic relationships
- Roadblocks that materialize from ego

Easier said than done, right? But it can be done. The key is realizing that we have a choice. Just as we can choose where to direct our energy, we can decide where not to direct it.

I often talk about *ego* or *earthly ego*, terms that I use interchangeably. I reference them loosely and not in a psychoanalytic or Freudian way. When I say *ego* or *earthly ego*, I am referring to the human mind rather than our soul's true essence. It's the part of us that has difficulty letting go of the need to control, and it plays a role in creating toxic roadblocks that can lead to emotional pain and dysfunctional relationships. Ego can separate us from the divine.

Letting go of transgressions can be challenging, especially for good people with a strong conscience. If we say or do something that hurts someone, it can stick with us for a long time — even if the hurt was unintentional and we've already apologized. Even when the person tells us to forget about it, that's not always easy. I don't necessarily think that's a bad quality. It's evidence of a kind heart and strong moral character. But being afraid or reluctant to accept our imperfections and move forward can be detrimental to our mental well-being. We must forgive ourselves, whether or not the other person forgives us. What the other person feels is their choice, but that does not change how we should feel about ourselves.

Our mistakes can be easily magnified today, more than ever before. We live in a society where our words and actions can be captured and instantly shared worldwide through social media and the internet. What we do and say can have lasting effects on how we are perceived. We are only human, and we make mistakes. We may even unintentionally hurt someone else and want to seek forgiveness. But before we can do that, we must let go of the need to be perfect. This is what I mean about needing to forgive ourselves. By letting go, we accept that we are not perfect, and we don't need the approval of others to feel whole. In doing this for ourselves, we also make space for the imperfections of others. We don't need to demand perfection from others because we don't demand it from ourselves.

Forgiving ourselves means knowing ourselves (including

our flaws), accepting what we cannot change, and changing what we can. My astrological sign is Virgo, which tends to be one of the more critical-minded signs in the zodiac. I sometimes need introspection to become aware of this impulse to be critical and then to change that language within my own mindset. Whenever I find myself focusing on my imperfections or those of others, I remind myself that this is my earthly ego running rampant. I know this expectation of perfection is unrealistic and only leads to suffering. I must let go of the need to control. If we can learn to overlook our own imperfections, we can learn to love others more fully, despite their flaws. We can love others for who they truly are, not for whether they live up to our expectations.

Actress Kristin Chenoweth once said, "If you can learn to love yourself and all the flaws, you can love other people so much better." It's true. Loving others, including their flaws, requires letting go of our own expectations of self-perfection. How could we expect to accept others for who they are if we don't accept ourselves?

But what if other people's flaws are harming us in some way? This leads to my next point: letting go of toxic relationships.

Toxic relationships can be the cause of unresolved emotional issues that can contribute to low self-worth. These are relationships that continually suck the joy out of us, lead us down the wrong path, or harm us mentally, physically, or emotionally. Many people have experienced a relationship like this, to one degree or another. However, we need to distinguish between what is toxic and what is a hindrance.

Our instant-gratification society is often quick to discard whatever seems no longer valuable. In some ways, we are living in an era of overconsumption and disposability. Maybe we un-friend a family member on social media because we don't share their political views, or we stop reaching out to an old friend because they don't respond to a text right away. We live in a culture in which people often go to an extreme by removing anyone from their lives who makes a mistake, disagrees with their views, doesn't make them happy all the time, or possesses annoying habits. We've become more impatient than ever be-fore, no doubt due to our diminishing attention spans. This is partly due to our smartphones and our exposure to the con-stant, twenty-four-hour news cycle and to social media plat-forms.

But willingly engaging with media is a choice. To keep our vibration high, we need to let go of the desire to keep up and absorb the continual dramas on our screens. This doesn't mean we should stop watching the news or cut people out of our lives. It means being cautious with what we allow ourselves to feed into. As humans, we are expected to coexist, help each other, love one another, and have tolerance. There are eight billion people on this planet, each with different perspectives, experi-ences, and emotional wounds. We need to remember that we don't always have the full picture as to why people are the way they are. Each person deals with a unique set of circumstances. Judging others for their behavior doesn't leave us room to grow in wisdom; it only blocks us from what otherwise could be meaningful relationships, despite our differences. When I talk about letting go, yes, it could mean letting go of a person for good. But it can also mean letting go of a particular mistake that person has made, a habit they have, or a personality trait that annoys us. We let go of our own intolerance, which often reflects our own insecurities.

In any relationship, romantic or otherwise, we are bound to encounter quirks about the other person that annoy us, just as we have quirks that bother others. Our ego tends to latch on to other people's flaws because it justifies a belief about ourselves that we are "better." But the truth is we're not; we're just different. For example, I have a friend who is always running late. At first, this behavior bothered me. Then, one day, I asked myself why I was so upset, and I realized that I felt disrespected, like my time wasn't valuable to this person. But that was my ego at work. There are so many things about my friend that I love, like her generosity and kindness. She's a real down-to-earth person. I feel I can be myself around her without judgment. Realizing that the reward I gain from the friendship far outweighs this flaw, I let go of the need to be right and accepted my friend for who she is. I let go of the expectations that she be different. Of course, if something important bothers us, we should express that. But what if the other person doesn't change, as was the case with my friend? We have the power to accept others with all of their idiosyncrasies and direct our energy instead toward what we love about them. If what we love about them outweighs what we don't, then we have our answer.

Here's a hypothetical example: Let's say a job interview goes very well, and as you wait for the decision, you want to share your excitement with someone you love. You call your sister, but she's a cautious, even pessimistic person. She responds by saying, "Well, I'm glad you're excited, but don't get your hopes up."

Pshhhhhhhhhhp! That's the sound of the air going out of your balloon. Just like that, your positive vibration is gone. You had set the intention to get this job before you scheduled the interview, you had confidently carried that intention into the interview, and you had maintained it afterward — until you called your sister. She did not intend to crush your spirit; she is just skeptical by nature. Do you need to let her go from your life? Of course not; she's your sister, and you love her. Is she toxic? No, that is too strong a word. But maybe the next time you are waiting on some potentially good news, you might wait to call her until the good news is official. In other words, we can set boundaries — such as by deciding when not to call someone for advice and support. We can remain close to people we love while managing our expectations and mindset in ways that allow us to maintain a good relationship.

Undoubtedly, some relationships are truly toxic and need to be dissolved. I've known people in relationships who are victims of abuse — physical, mental, or emotional. While the choice to leave isn't always cut and dry, especially when safety is an issue, leaving a hurtful person can be necessary. For me, my mom is an example. She had to leave my dad to survive, and she took an enormous risk doing so, especially by taking me with her, but she finally did it. She didn't have the best life after she left him, but I know it was better than if she had stayed — better for both of them and likely for me.

Social media is one of those places where letting go is a muddy topic. People with different viewpoints (especially political ones) often are quick to dismiss each other, even if they have been face-to-face friends for years. It almost defies logic, but it has become a common occurrence. This is sad, and to me it exemplifies our current era of disposability. It doesn't need to be that way, though. We can change if we set the intention to think differently about others — with more compassion and empathy. I've found that, like anything, if we use social media for the right intention — to stay connected to people and to be motivated and inspired — it can enrich our life. This is why, many years ago, I started posting inspirational messages on Facebook. I just wanted people to have some positivity throughout their day. Because my intention was pure, my following grew, and to this day, I receive countless messages of gratitude from people worldwide about how these posts help them change their thinking and raise their vibration. This is the purpose these social media platforms should serve — to uplift and connect people. They are not always used in that way, and it's unfortunate because the potential to reach people for the purpose of healing is boundless.

If you feel like all you see when you log on is toxic behavior, remember that you can choose not to let that energy into you. To quote Don Miguel Ruiz in *The Four Agreements*, "Someone can intentionally send emotional poison, and if you don't take it personally, you will not eat it. When you don't take the emotional poison, it becomes even worse to the sender, but not in you." You don't need to let go of friends or family members with whom you disagree. Instead, you can send them love, surround them in white light, and stop clicking on their posts! It's truly amazing what happens when we send love to someone who spews venom outwardly. They will either change on their own in time or go away altogether. Let go of the need to change other people. It's not your burden to bear.

Everyone has quirks and personality traits that don't jive with ours. That's part of the human condition, and we should tolerate others who are different from us. But sometimes a relationship can go beyond what we can, or should have to, handle. Each of us is trying to create our version of heaven here on earth, to live our best life. When somebody we are associated with doesn't have that same attitude, it's not a "vibrational match," as I like to call it. That is when, for our well-being, we need to consider a change. It is similar to the philosophy of Marie Kondo, author of *The Life-Changing Magic of Tidying Up*. We keep only those items — or in this case, those people — that speak to the heart, and we let go of those that do not bring us joy.

As another example, consider a relationship where one person is an alcoholic and the other is sober. Why would the sober person put up with the self-destructive addictive behavior of the other? Love and a desire to help are two reasons. Many people can get trapped in the viscous cycle of addiction and need help to overcome it, and they may not realize the damage they are causing their partner. But if the sober person comes to feel powerless, alone, and hopeless, and if, despite being told what's wrong or hurtful, the addicted person refuses to change their negative behavior or be helped, then the relationship is not good for either person. It is no longer serving either person's highest good. It is not our job to save someone else. We cannot let the destructive behavior of others become roadblocks to our own happiness.

Another aspect of letting go is releasing all roadblocks that materialize from ego. This one is tricky because it requires us to let go of rational thought — our ego — in order to reach our greatest potential, which we achieve through access to our higher or intuitive self.

When we let our ego take over, we can only see things through a rational lens. What is wrong with that? Nothing, if we're working on math equations or scientific theories. The rational ego mind is very good at organizing things into patterns. But the rational mind can limit our thinking by shutting out the spiritual side of our being, essentially blocking us from an entire realm of potential possibility. With our earthly ego, we tend to have an attitude that it's our way or no way, which can lead to tunnel vision. Ironically, this can also lead to irrational thinking. Our ego feels the need to control the outcome. But if we work toward letting go of control, Spirit can direct us toward our goals in the most mysterious and glorious ways possible. This is why I always say to expect the unexpected. It is in letting go that we make room for what we didn't know we needed. When we think from our intuitive side — our creative and spiritual side — we feel limitless, like anything is possible. We tend to feel it's okay to let go and trust the process, that time is not a factor. This is how trust in our intuition can grow. Everything happens as it should when we allow our intuitive side to work in conjunction with our rational ego. This is the balance between the body and the soul, which completes us and makes us whole.

As an example of ego getting in the way, consider a budding actor who has just arrived in Hollywood, which is not an easy place to survive. The actor only has experience in his hometown's community theater, where he was a local celebrity, so he declines minor roles because they don't fit how he sees himself — as a star. This narrative, created by his earthly ego, keeps him from accepting the work he finds, and so he ends up like many aspiring actors — unemployed and lost in a sea of competing talent. But if he accepted where he was at in his life at that moment, let go of the need for perfection, and cast a net of attraction out into the Universe, he would build the connections he needs in his journey to being "discovered." He would also develop the craft of acting, which would improve his chances of success. With this mindset, he would attract greater opportunity.

Something similar happened to a neighbor of mine, who asked me for guidance regarding her job search. She had been unemployed for about a year but had a wealth of experience in the IT sector as a software analyst. She had hastily quit her previous job because she had grown tired of being rejected every time she applied for a leadership position within her company. She wanted to make a change and seek a promotion outside the company. However, the impulsiveness of her decision to leave caught up to her, as she was unemployed for quite some time. She applied to several companies within her industry but kept getting rejected. With the guidance I received from Spirit, I informed her that she would be offered a position soon and should take it. Even if it wasn't exactly what she wanted, it would be an excellent opportunity to get her foot in the door and grow within the company. It would also allow her to continue searching for exactly what she wanted while still earning a paycheck. Days after our meeting, she was offered a position at a company in Silicon Valley. She was excited about this change. It was the company she really wanted to work for and an opportunity to live somewhere she had always dreamed of living. But she wasn't happy with the job title, so she asked them to change it from a department manager to a director. Days later, she received an email saying they had elected to move forward without her. Unfortunately, after that, my neighbor was back to square one and struggled to find another job. This is another lesson in letting go, both of the need to control outcomes and of wanting to fulfill our expectations exactly. Sometimes, we have to acclimate ourselves to a new environment, or slowly gain the necessary skills, experience, and connections, to reach the places we want. Like anything else, letting go is about taking the plunge into the unknown.

Many of us have difficulty letting go, especially when it involves loss. We might hold on to the emotional pain of a loved one passing or the end of a relationship, as if holding on somehow keeps the person with us. But letting go doesn't mean avoidance; it means allowing ourselves to be imperfect and exist with our emotions. With loss, emotions are like a wave that moves through us. Fighting this wave only makes the struggle more challenging. We must let go and ride it to get over the top. We let go of what we cannot change and have faith that we are divinely connected. Letting go of what doesn't serve us is hard work, but it allows us to make room for what does serve us. It means we recognize that we have the power to decide how to look at what is before us. Is the wave going to drown us, or can we make it over the top? How we choose to think about a hurdle can profoundly impact whether we overcome it. Letting go of what no longer serves us means trusting ourselves and trusting in our divine connection to the other side. This recognition is a significant part of awakening.

DAILY PRACTICE

Letting Go Using the Flame of Transformation

Through meditative visualization, we let go of all the accumulated "stuff" that no longer serves us. By burning away all that is unwanted, we transmute it back into the Universe for repurposing and renewal, which is the fate of all things. In letting go, we take our power back to forge a new path in life without limitations.

Focus solely on your breath. Breathe in slowly and hold it for a second, feeling the expanse of your belly and rib cage. Now slowly exhale. Send out with your breath everything on your mind, releasing the unnecessary worries of the day. Repeat this until you are comfortable and in a relaxed state. See yourself standing alone on a beach at sunset. It is your private space for reflection. The sand is soft and warm between your toes as the waves crash on the shore. In the distance, a firepit burns bright with a magical pink flame, like nothing you've ever seen before. This light brings you joy. It calls to you. You feel safe here.

Next, imagine yourself holding a sturdy leather bag with strong leather handles. Nothing can get out once it's inside. Open the bag and place it on the ground. Visualize that you have a magic wand in your hand. This wand can shrink anything so that it fits inside the bag. Sit for a moment and contemplate all the things you are ready to release. Once you are ready, visualize at least one item you have wanted to let go of for a long time. This may be as simple as clutter in your home or as complex as a relationship that no longer serves you. Intently visualize this item — the object or person and any of its characteristics, such as the shape, feel, or smell. Now tap this with your wand to shrink the item and place it in the bag. As you do, take a deep breath and release it fully, so that you feel lighter.

If you need to let go of something intangible, like an emotion that no longer serves you, imagine this emotion as a ball of fire hovering in the air. Point the wand at it, shrink it to the size of a marble, then drop it into the bag. Repeat these steps as many times as you need with as many items as necessary.

Once your bag is full, pick it up and carry it to the firepit. With each step, the bag becomes heavier and heavier, weighing you down, reminding you of the weight in your heart you have been carrying for so long. When you reach the fire, drop the bag into it. Back up to gain perspective on what you have just released. Watch the bag burn, hear the embers crackle, and watch the energy within all the items in the bag transform into smoke, which dissipates into the air.

Release, remove, and let go of that which no longer serves you as it transmutes back into the Universe for renewal. Feel lighter now as you open to new beginnings and get ready to move forward with new, positive energy.

Chapter 3

FORGIVENESS

Forgiveness is the fragrance that the violet sheds
on the heel that has crushed it.

— MARK TWAIN

There may be nothing more difficult in this world than to forgive someone who has wronged us. There also may be nothing more freeing than forgiveness. Whether to forgive someone or not is a choice, which means we are in control, even if we feel we are not. Forgiveness does not equate to exoneration. It does not mean the forgiven person is now our friend, although that's possible. We are not soft for offering mercy, and forgiveness can also take years. But no matter how long it takes, the reward is powerful because it frees our soul from the burden of victimization.

I've journeyed my path of forgiveness in life. My relationship with my dad over the years has been complicated. I love him, but I didn't get to a place of peace in my heart overnight.

I went through a lot of soul searching, and it took time to get to where we are now. While growing up, I saw things no child should see because of my parents. How my dad treated my mom was often terrible; he could be a vengeful bully. When I was nine years old, after I was brought back to the West Coast, he wouldn't let me go to New York to visit my mom out of spite toward her. Yes, I had regular phone calls with her, but I was kept from seeing her. I realize now that both of my parents used me as a form of punishment for each other. I did not see my mother once from when I was nine until her death six years later. At the time, I was angry at my dad for this.

Through readings with clients, deep meditations, and various experiences over the years, I have learned from Spirit that we are on earth to learn lessons about love and forgiveness. These lessons about forgiveness are a catalyst for experiencing unconditional love. Even though I went through what I did while growing up, I know on a soul level that this was predestined. My parents have their own life lessons that they came here to learn, but on a soul level, they also chose the roles they did in my life — to aid in my experience — so that I would have greater empathy and compassion for people in need. So, as hard as it may be to accept, any heartache you've experienced, any wrongdoings against you, and any pain inflicted by those you love most were all orchestrated on the other side before you entered this life. There is a grand design for your soul's purpose and evolution while you're here.

My work to rebuild my relationship with my dad has also changed *him*. We still have our disagreements about the reality of what happened in my childhood, but mutual respect and love have materialized over time. Even though he hasn't apologized directly to me for all the pain and hurt his behavior caused, he has made huge strides toward owning up to his role in what I went through. This is a prime example of how we don't always need someone to apologize to forgive them.

Much like how hate can be contagious, forgiveness can also spread and flow through people's hearts because of the intention behind it. Don't you feel inspired when you see someone forgiving someone else who has wronged them? We feel like we could do the same. We don't need to be the victim to justify the "crime." People who experience abuse know precisely what this means: The strength we find comes in taking the higher road, and we can walk that road confidently with our head held high because we can let go of the need to be right or acknowledged by somebody else. We already have our own sense of self-worth. And when we have that, we can begin to forgive. Forgiving my dad enabled him to open his heart more. We have a relationship now. Is it perfect? No, but it is stronger than it has ever been.

When we hold on to resentment, we carry the heavy burden of the broken relationship on our shoulders, which prevents us from healing. Forgiving makes it easier to move forward. We are no longer constrained by the negative thoughts we have of that person. Releasing this resentment makes room for new prospects and allows us to reclaim the happiness and positivity that we deserve in our life.

I have a client who, over the years, has become a dear friend of mine. In the past, his wife had cheated on him and put them in financial debt, and because of his understandable bitterness, he divorced her. He first came to me because his lingering anger over this was creating numerous roadblocks in his life. It affected his relationships and ultimately hurt his ability to run his business, causing anxiety and depression. He needed to find a way past these feelings. What was interesting was that, when he and I first met, it had been many years since his divorce. This is why I say wounds can take time to heal, but forgiveness is still necessary. As long as he held on to his resentment, it would affect other aspects of his life.

I talked to him about forgiving his ex. He had never considered it because he saw forgiveness as something he'd do for her, not for himself. He also thought it would be an indirect way of saying that what she had done to him was okay. Plus, he assumed forgiveness required saying the words verbally and directly, so she heard them. I explained that none of that was true. If he could find a way in his heart and mind to forgive her, it would not necessarily set her free; it would set him free. If he decided to tell her directly, and if that set her free, too, then so be it. But that would have no bearing on what it would do for him, which was the focus — *his* well-being. It took him some time and deep reflection, but he finally did it. After he did, he told me that he felt lighter. The weight had been lifted. It was like the cork had popped off a champagne bottle, and the bubbly was released and flowing again in his life. He was no longer fighting the current. He was back in alignment with his greater purpose.

I understand there are situations when forgiveness feels impossible, especially if actions lead to a fatality or an injustice that sends a person's life into a downward spiral. I've heard people say, "What he did to me is unforgivable!" This is an understandable response. But what I've learned through my own experience is that we have the power to make peace with even the most unforgivable of situations, or at least head in that direction, so that maybe one day we can ultimately reach forgiveness.

One of the most powerful stories I've read about forgiveness involves a woman named Missy Jenkins Smith. Missy was fifteen years old in 1997 when she was one of eight students shot by a fourteen-year-old classmate at Heath High School in Paducah, Kentucky. Three students were killed, and among the five who survived, Missy was the most seriously injured, paralyzed from the chest down. The boy who shot her was a friend, someone Missy knew from band. He was not aiming for her; he was firing indiscriminately in the lobby before classes that morning, and he changed Missy's life forever. Before the shooting, Missy was a typical teenage girl who played soccer and was in the marching band. Now, she'd never again have the use of her legs.

On the day of the shooting, while Missy was in the hospital, she stunned her family by telling them that she'd already forgiven the shooter. As to *how* she did it, she says in her book *I Choose to Be Happy*: "It may sound bizarre that a fifteen-year-old could think that way, but I did. Maybe it stemmed from my baptism less than two years earlier in the eighth grade. That momentous night in front of that congregation had strengthened my faith to the point where, as a teenager, my relationship with God was as strong as it had ever been."

As to *why* she did it, Missy says: "I needed to forgive him for me if I were going to get past that tragic day and make something of my life. I was able to free my heart of any anger I had toward [him] and move forward. I hoped that forgiving him had a positive effect on him. But the forgiveness was mainly for me."

After the shooting, Missy returned to high school to graduate, earned a college degree in social work, married, had two children, and worked as a school counselor. She shares her story nationwide each year with thousands of schoolchildren and focuses on several lessons, one of them being the power of forgiveness. She even initiated a visit with the shooter in prison ten years later to talk about what happened and to tell him face-to-face that she forgave him.

I'm sure many people would never expect Missy to forgive the shooter, and certainly not to forgive him on the same day he paralyzed her. But Missy was already profoundly connected to Spirit through her faith when the shooting happened. While her declaration was a shock to the rest of the world, it made sense to her because of the link she had established with a higher power. Wise beyond her years, she knew that the key to overcoming the physical and mental obstacles she was about to face began with forgiveness. Forgiveness enabled her to push forward and take control of her new situation, despite the challenging days ahead as she adjusted to her new life.

Whether or not you choose to forgive is entirely up to you and nobody else. Your pain and wounds belong to you alone and are yours to hold on to if you choose. But like clutter in a junk drawer, they take up space in your life. You must ask yourself, *Do these emotional wounds serve me today?*

I choose to forgive because of what it does for my soul and the freedom it affords me emotionally. Think about Missy and the injustices imposed upon her. She had every right never to forgive the boy who hurt her, but she decided to look at it differently — to go down the less-traveled road. To quote the great poet Robert Frost, "Two roads diverged in a wood, and I — I took the one less traveled by, and that has made all the difference." Ask yourself: Are you genuinely happy, or are you holding on to past hurts and find yourself stuck at a crossroads, unsure of which way to go? In this moment, at any moment, you have an opportunity to choose: to stick with the status quo and the familiar path (of holding on to pain) or of taking the less-traveled road, to forgive and let go. Who knows what new possibilities await you in your personal growth, around that unseeable bend in the road?

DAILY PRACTICE

Your Sanctuary of Forgiveness

Through meditation, we can choose to forgive those we feel have wronged us — for the purpose of healing ourselves. This releases us from energies of the past that weigh us down so that we can move forward. Water not only cleanses us physically but metaphorically. It is representative of our emotional state and is symbolic of new beginnings — clearing away the emotional "dirt" of the past.

Sit in a comfortable position and close your eyes. If you have someone in your life who you have not been able to forgive, this is the opportunity to release them from holding space within you. Focus on your breath and allow yourself to go deeper within with every breath. Visualize this person standing in front of you. See their face. As you inhale, feel yourself become heavier and heavier. Pull this unresolved energy into your solar plexus, the area right below your diaphragm and above your navel. As you exhale, feel the heaviness escape you and dissipate into the air. Continue this breathing exercise until you feel completely relaxed. You have entered your sacred inner world.

This world is your sanctuary. Visualize being outside in nature. You feel safe here. It is nighttime, but the moon is full and shines brightly down onto this natural setting. You are

comfortable as you stand bare in front of the most beautiful waterfall of flowing light. The reflection of the moonlight
is charging this liquid light as it powerfully flows down into
a pure, clear creek surrounded by pink crystals. A powerful
beam of love emanates from these crystals. This is unconditional love. It floods you like a loving entity calling to you. You
realize this magical waterfall of light is there to heal all the
emotional wounds you have carried with you for so long.

Approach the waterfall. As each crystal-charged sprinkle
of water lands on you, it melts away any unforgiving energy
within, any wrongdoings that you are consciously and subcon-
sciously holding. Your inner light, once dimmed by emotional
pain, now becomes brighter. As this powerful water draws you
nearer, you feel old pains come up. Old resentments and fears
bubble to the surface, but there are no cracks or corners for
the pain to hide in as it is flooded with this magical water light.
Finally, step into the waterfall, allowing it to pour over your
skin. Be gentle with yourself at this moment. Allow this energy
to move through you. It's been there for so long. This magical
light water carries that all away from you now. Let go.

Feel this light entering your body on a cellular level, reaching your soul. There is an intense rush through your heart's
center. The energy is so healing, like nothing you've ever experienced before. You feel safe and supported. You surrender to
the light and allow yourself to merge with it, feeling free and
weightless. The pink light of the crystals emanates through the
creek bed. The light is so clear, vivid, and bright. Say out loud
as many times as you feel necessary, "I forgive you." Feel a
renewed sense of well-being. There are new possibilities in
store for you. Know that you can always return to this scene
to heal wounds that arise or simply for inspiration to forgive
and move forward.

Chapter 4

THE THOUGHT TRANSFORMATION

All problems are illusions of the mind.

— ECKHART TOLLE

Many things in this world are out of our control — natural disasters, political instabilities, and even our physical mortality. But there is one thing we can take control of: our thoughts. It's not always easy, but it is always possible.

The energy from the thoughts we allow to run rampant in our minds profoundly influences our relationship with the world and others. How often do we lose sleep because we worry about issues beyond our control? Or replay negative conversations in our minds? Or imagine worst-case scenarios that likely will never happen? These thoughts come from our earthly ego, which tends to dominate our minds. On a human level, they may help us sort through what went right or wrong, how to do better next time, or how to prepare for something unknown. But the way our minds wander can lead us down rabbit holes with dead ends. Fortunately, we can reprogram our thoughts to be more loving, productive, and healthy for ourselves and those around us.

When I was a senior at the San Francisco Conservatory of Music, I had my own personal experience with the power of thought transformation. I was in a tough position because I didn't have enough money to pay my tuition. At this time in my life, I felt alone and disconnected from my family; they were hundreds of miles away in Southern California. After I came out of the closet with my grandma, my daily calls with her turned into weekly calls and eventually monthly calls. She had difficulty understanding this part of me because of her Christian faith. I felt like I was on my own, and I went to bed each night and woke up each morning worried about what would happen. I was afraid that I wouldn't graduate. My situation triggered a lot of unresolved issues from my childhood, including feelings of loneliness and abandonment. Instability made me feel unsafe. I feared that I would lose everything I had worked so hard to achieve and be left with nothing.

I decided to try a manifestation experiment. A classmate at the conservatory, Brittany, who has since become an invaluable friend, could not stop talking about a documentary she had watched called *The Secret*. The film, later a book, had taken the world by storm, so she brought it over one day and we watched it together. The film centers around how to bring about positive change in our lives and how to vibrate at the same frequency as our wants and desires in order to let go of what no longer serves us. This is accomplished by being conscious of our thoughts and the words we use, internally and out loud. By intention-setting through practice and repetition, we can change the way we think and manifest our desires. This was exactly what I needed to hear at that moment in my life. I look back at this time, which was filled with uncertainty and disconnection from my family, and I have gratitude in my heart for the friends and support network I was building. They would lead me down the path I was meant to be on toward my greater purpose in life.

Although I was pursuing a music degree, I was also deeply entrenched in my spiritual growth. I had started to develop a strong connection to the other side in these formative years. After watching *The Secret*, I realized the only way that I could graduate, given my circumstances, was to surrender. I had to let go and ask for help from my spirit guides more than ever before. By asking for support from the other side, I recognized something greater in my life. This idea of the invisible world working to assist me quickly became a profound comfort in a difficult time. I remembered my experience on the bus as a child and how I called upon the white light for protection and safety, and I felt it was important to call upon that power again to assist me with this situation.

One morning on my way to school, I was sitting on a bus in the Sunset district in San Francisco. Unable to shake my fears and worries about my situation, I put on my headphones and listened to Mozart to tune out the outside world. I took this moment of solitude to thank the Universe, my guides, my mom, and all the people on the other side (what I refer to as our "spiritual web"; see chapter 10) for helping me try to find a way to finish my degree. I visualized the exact amount of money I needed — twenty-five thousand dollars — and I surrounded this image in a glow of white light. I then visualized myself at my graduation ceremony in my cap and gown with my diploma in hand. I spent about five minutes in this deep meditative state.

The overwhelming feeling of support and peace I felt after this inspired me to keep at it, and I made it part of my daily practice. I know in my heart that my mom has always worked effortlessly from heaven to nudge me down the right path in life. As I continued to practice this visualization, I sensed my mom's embrace, which further empowered me to keep doing it. Each day I finished my meditative visualization practice by reminding myself to let go of "how" and "when." Releasing the need to control was challenging, but I felt more liberated each time I let go and asked for support from the other side. Although I had let go of how and when, I always kept the dollar amount I needed in my mind's eye whenever I practiced. I felt it was important to visualize the exact amount, to bring energy to my intention. This visualization technique was the start of the meditative practices that I continue to use today.

I practiced this ritual for about three weeks until, one morning, I received a call from Debra, the financial aid counselor at my school. She said she needed to discuss something with me and asked me to come to her office. The negative thoughts that I'd managed to keep at bay for the past few weeks reemerged. When I hung up the phone with her, I felt fear slip. My earthly ego took control of my mind again. My heart was pounding, and I could feel tiny beads of sweat gathering on my forehead. *This is it. They're going to kick me out*, I said to myself. We were in the first week of October, about six weeks into the school year, and I had a large balance due on my tuition fees. But I also felt a sense of excitement that I couldn't quite place. It was like a sense of hope in my heart — if I were meant to finish what I had started, a miracle would occur.

As I walked through the heavy San Francisco morning fog to Debra's office, I tried to compose myself and gather my thoughts. When I entered the bustling halls of the conservatory, I didn't want to imagine a world in which I was unable to finish my time there and would have to leave this extraordinary place I loved so much. With each step I took up those stairs to the administration office, I reminded myself of the peace I'd found in my meditative practice over the last few weeks. As I walked, I decided that I needed to be okay with whatever was meant to be for me. I had to surrender again.

When I arrived, Debra invited me in and closed the door. "Bill, I have some news for you. You're going to want to sit down for this." With my heart racing, I could barely feel my hands grip the chair as I stumbled into my seat.

"We have had a very generous donor gift a significant amount of money to the conservatory. They've asked that we divvy it up to a few of the most deserving students here. We all agree that we want you to be one of those students. We have twenty-five thousand dollars for you, which will cover your tuition for the rest of year."

I was shaking as I dropped my head and sobbed. I was in a state of overwhelming disbelief, gratitude, and relief. It had worked; my manifestation practice had paid off, literally. I went from thinking my days at the conservatory were numbered to learning that I was going to graduate in about seven months with the degree I'd worked so hard to earn. After thanking Debra for this tremendous honor, hugging her, and gathering myself, I left her office.

While walking outside, I saw the fog had lifted, and the sun was shining bright. At that moment, I heard a voice in my head say, *See, I told you everything would be fine.* I felt a warmth of loving support wash over me. I couldn't stop thinking about how powerful my visualization practice had been. I knew that, going forward, this way of thinking would become a part of my life forever. By taking control of my thoughts through intention-setting, I manifested what I needed. There is power in this positive and even "magical" thinking — a power that can bring the reality you desire to fruition, so long as it aligns with the highest good of all.

This begs the question: If that donor hadn't stepped up, would my spiritual effort have been deemed a failure?

Not at all.

It worked out the way it did because the intention I set aligned with the intention the school set to donate money to a deserving student. Another reason my intention worked was that I left the how and when open. By leaving this broader, I allowed the result to manifest by whatever path was easiest. Even if that money hadn't come through in that manner, I still set my intention to stay in school and graduate. My eye was on the prize, and by whatever means possible, it was going to happen, so long as it was in the highest good for all. Maybe I would have found a bank to loan me the money, or the school would have developed some other plan for me to pay the tuition over time after I graduated. I believed my intention would become my reality in some form, and it did. Perhaps the most profound outcome of the whole situation was that I found faith.

When your intention is to manifest something for a greater purpose, for all involved, there's no limit to what you can create for yourself. The reason that my desire to manifest staying at the school worked out was because it lined up with the desires of the school. They didn't want to lose me; that was their intention as well. When you have a passion and excitement for something, an activation occurs within you because you are connected to your source energy. This is being in alignment with Spirit, your purpose, and your gifts. Even if the excitement you feel is fleeting, it is true at the time. These moments are like little bread crumbs leading you down the road to where you belong. There is power in this excitement and momentum, in believing in something greater than you. When you control your thoughts, connect to your spiritual side, and align with what you want and what's in everyone's best interests, the chances of achieving your intention increase exponentially.

This doesn't mean that the issue we're dealing with goes away when we take control of our thoughts. If we need money for tuition, then we need money for tuition; that doesn't change. But what we've done is change the dialogue. When we repeat something (positive or negative), it has a way of sticking. Our soul works similarly. If we do that inner work and reprogram our thoughts from negative to positive, it takes away our fear and puts us on a path toward happiness.

Here's another example. Let's say a woman named Maggie finds out that her husband cheated on her with another woman. The infidelity leaves her devastated, and she eventually divorces her husband. While Maggie knows deep down that her ex-husband is to blame, she can't help but feel insecure and depressed, even finding reasons to blame herself for their breakup. She feels isolated, loses confidence, and questions her intelligence and physical looks. *If my husband rejected me, so will everyone else*, Maggie thinks. At first, she chooses to remain depressed, and this may serve a purpose for a while as she moves through the grief. But eventually, Maggie needs to take control of her thoughts and change her inner dialogue to exit a negative cycle of thinking that is damaging her self-worth.

To do this, Maggie decides to write down everything negative about herself that has been running rampant through her mind since she and her husband split up. She writes down things like "I have no confidence," "I'm not very attractive," and "I am to blame for what he did to me." The more she puts her thoughts down on paper and *sees* them, the more difficult it becomes to write the next thought because she can see how absurd it is. We don't always pay attention to or recall every thought that crosses our minds, but the reality is that these thoughts — when allowed to repeat endlessly — have damaging effects on our well-being. All it takes is a trigger from the outside world to send us into a negative thought spiral. We must break the energy behind this cycle through positive affirmation. Maggie hadn't really changed since she was married; she was still a confident, intelligent, attractive, and honest woman. On a deeper level, she knew this to be true. But by allowing the negative narrative in her mind to run rampant, it had consumed her.

Maggie's next step, after writing down all the negative thoughts, is to rewrite them as positive phrases, like "I am confident!" "I am attractive!" and "I am a loving and faithful partner!" As this changes the dialogue in her mind, her attitude toward herself begins to change. She wakes up each morning and puts on clothes that make her feel good. She calls girlfriends to get together to maintain her social life and make new connections. She makes a conscious effort to smile more and pamper herself. Before long, she regains enough confidence to explore dating again.

Writing down her thoughts doesn't immediately eradicate Maggie's fear of change, but it helps her rediscover who she is. It is a significant step forward and opens the door to break the negative cycle she's fallen into. By confronting her negative thought patterns and taking time for self-care, Maggie connects to her higher source. She could easily sit in front of the television and escape, use drugs to numb the pain, and nurture her anger at her ex-husband. Instead, Maggie chooses to take a hard look at how her thoughts are dominating her, and she takes steps to change those thoughts, which allows an entirely new world of possibilities into her life.

Thoughts lead to action. This is how they can tear down a society or build it up, ultimately shaping the world in which we live. The choice is ours. Admittedly, I am an optimist. I've always been this way, despite my rocky childhood. Making it through those challenging times shaped my outlook and forced me to recognize the influence of my thought patterns early. Because there was so much paranoia and fearful thinking around me, I was always working on improving what I had control over, which were my thoughts. So, I spent time praying to God. This was my powerful tool of survival.

We can make it through anything with the right approach and attitude. But the wrong approach and attitude can have the polar opposite effect. This is why we must be careful with what we think and speak. It's easy to get sucked into a negative feedback loop, whether because of something serious that's happened to us or because of general fears about the unknown. We need to realize that if we fall into the trap of negative thinking, we have the power to "flip the negatives," as I like to call it. When we flip the energy of negative thought, we regain control of our state of being and begin a new chapter with positive outcomes.

DAILY PRACTICE

Flipping the Negatives and Accessing Your Higher Self

In this writing exercise, you practice breaking the cycle of negative thought patterns by writing your negative thoughts down and rewriting them with their positive opposites. Writing them down is important because it forces us to face them in an irrefutable way.

Find a quiet space where you will not be disturbed. I like to create a mood in my environment by lighting incense or burning palo santo or sage to clear the energy of the space. For this practice, also have some loose pieces of paper and a pen.

Start with a simple breathing exercise. Take a deep breath and say the word *peace* on the inhale, then say the word *still* on the exhale. Use this as your mantra for building your connection to Spirit. Do this as many times as you need until you feel completely relaxed and stillness permeates your physical body. Your breath should be natural and flow comfortably and continuously. Now say to yourself, *I connect with my higher self to aid me in this spiritual practice.*

Bring forth any negative thoughts that you feel are holding you back in your life and from your highest good. Be honest. Then write down these negative thoughts, the ones that consume you. Make sure to leave space between each statement on the page. As you write, you may feel a pull in your heart chakra, and that's okay. You're opening this center of your emotional body to allow healing. (See the appendix for an explanation of the chakras.) Don't edit anything. Keep writing negative thoughts until you feel a purge has occurred; you may notice a shift in you from this release. Then read what you have written and notice the narrative that reveals itself about the person who has these fears and worries. This is the old story — the old belief of yourself. Take a long look at this. Allow the emotions to arise. You may hear a voice within that reflects upon this narrative with empathy. This is your higher self reaching out to you. You're now ready to go through each statement and flip the energy by writing your positives.

Turn your page of negative statements upside down. Above each negative statement, write a new positive version of that statement. These are loving and supportive statements that replace the old thoughts. You may notice that your positive statements embody a stronger voice with more substance. You are literally writing the statements in the opposite direction of the old ones. This gives energy to the new direction you are headed in, reinforcing a new belief system. As you write the positives, you may feel a pull in your solar plexus. This is where we hold older emotional pains and wounds that we've believed about ourselves and have not let go of or recognized. You are opening the solar plexus by facing these old emotional wounds, unblocking years of stagnation. When you finish, read these positive statements and notice the new narrative that comes to light. This is you. This is your higher self. You have now revealed the two sides of yourself, the earthly ego and the spirit self. By writing a new narrative, a more positive version of your thoughts, you are now plugged in to the divine energy source of the Universe. You are ready to start harnessing this power to forge your new path in life, to manifest the life you want.

DAILY PRACTICE

Manifesting Your Desires

This visualization is focused on manifesting your desired intentions. If you want, you can do this practice immediately after the practice above. Once you've flipped the negatives into positives and connected with your higher self, your vibration is high, and you are in the right space for manifestation. But if you need time to process the previous practice, you can do this one another day.

Bring to the forefront of your mind what you seek to manifest. Keep this intention to yourself so that it isn't influenced by others. Your desires are sacred. You want to keep them close to your heart, as there is more clear power this way, unaffected by the energy of others. This is something you have a deep, burning desire for in your life. Make sure it is for your highest good and for the highest good of all those involved. Keep the intention broad so that you're not limiting the how and when. Let go of timelines for the outcome. This is a practice in surrendering as well. It's important to visualize your intention as often as possible, ideally as a daily ritual, until you see the results. As you go about your life, remain open to how things materialize from your manifestation visualization. We cannot control how a manifestation unfolds. Trust that events will align as they are meant to be.

While in your sacred comfortable space, envision yourself in the situation you seek. Absorb it in every sense possible. See it. Smell it. Feel it. Identify with it however you can. Experience this intention as if it is happening in the present moment. It's not a wish. It's real to you. Once you have the visualization in your mind's eye, surround this image with a golden white light that enters through the top of your head (where the crown chakra resides). This is the light of source energy filling you. Call upon your spirit guides to assist you in your manifestation process. You're supported by the invisible world and empowered by the energy from Spirit. If you sense ego-based thoughts creeping in, remember to flip them to a positive, as in the previous practice. Give gratitude for all that you have at this moment. End the practice by saying, "Thank you."

This entire visualization practice might only take a few minutes, perhaps five to ten minutes, or it could be longer depending on what feels best to you.

Chapter 5

THE EVERLASTING POWER
IN WORDS

*What I know for sure: Words matter. And when they're written
and not just spoken, they last forever.*

— OPRAH WINFREY

Chapter 4 addresses the power of our thoughts and how they affect us personally. But what about speech, the words we say out loud? There are just twenty-six letters in the English alphabet, and they don't amount to much individually. But when properly arranged, they can have lasting effects on behavior, attitude, and self-worth. Most conflict in the world stems from the negative words people use to attack others. This is the earthly ego at its worst.

Don Miguel Ruiz, author of *The Four Agreements*, talks about the power our words have to lift others up or tear them down. This concept is important because, not only do our words hold immense power, but they reflect a lot about us as a person.

That can be good or bad, depending on intent. We need to ask ourselves what our intention is with the words we use.

With today's technology, words can be recorded and shared instantly with the entire world, whether in a text, video, audio recording, or social media post. These words have the potential to remain imprinted forever, but they are also stored in our minds and the minds of others. We can all recall when someone said something negative to us when we were children. Perhaps an adult yelled at us, or a kid at school used words to bully us. Words stick, and negative ones tend to stick more firmly than positive ones — even for a lifetime. This is because our ego mind latches onto negative words and comments more easily, since the critical mind seeks validation externally. Every time we say something out loud, our thoughts enter the world with lasting effects.

When we speak, we are deciding to affirm our thoughts out loud. If our thoughts are not in the best interests of those we are speaking to, what value do those thoughts have in the conversation? They are coming from a place of ego. This is what we want to be careful of — the ego-driven thoughts that spread our own fears, worries, and other negative emotions. The ego is terrified of being alone, so it tries to pull others along. What's important to understand is that our words are sending our inner world outward.

When speaking, keep in mind the saying, "We reap what we sow." In other words, if we spread fear or treat others unkindly, we can expect to receive the same. The energy we put out comes back to us, positive and negative. The words we use with others ultimately affect how we feel about ourselves. In our modern world, with the influence of the internet, this has never been truer. Words shared on the internet can be available for all to see, permanently in some cases, so how do you want to be remembered when you are no longer here in life? What do your words say about you?

Have you noticed that when you frequently comment on someone's social media posts, that person's posts start popping up more frequently in your feed? This is by design. Website algorithms are programmed to show us more of what we demonstrate interest in. The more we interact with certain posts — and certain words — the more of the same we receive. If what we respond to most often is negative, we will get more negative posts in our feed. If it's positive, we'll receive more positive posts. Our minds work the same way. If we spend most of our time arguing with people, we will continually attract more arguments into our life. People who spread negativity tend to attract negativity in all areas of life because that's the energetic vibration they're setting for themselves.

To set the energetic vibration for positive attraction, I start my day with an affirmation. This can be verbal or written. The first thing I do is say, "Thank you for this day." Then I add present-tense statements, which are usually different each day. It's essential to use present tense in affirmations because that reinforces the manifestation by removing it from an unattainable moment, the future. A positive statement can be simple, such as, "Today is filled with blessings. I navigate my day with ease and have positive interactions with others."

When I think of the power of speaking positive affirmations, I am reminded of what it took for me to finally tell the world about my gift. I spent time listening to the guidance I received from Spirit about what my path as a psychic medium meant to me and those in need of receiving messages. I had to do a lot of work with affirmations to get there. Mediumship was not nearly as mainstream as it is today. It took a lot of courage to publicly announce who I was. Whenever the ego voice slipped in and I doubted or feared what the reaction would be from the people in my life, I heard Spirit echoing in the background, *You are strong and capable. You are here to heal. You are a messenger.* I utilized these as my affirmations, inspired by my guides on the other side. This provided me with a sense of peace and reassurance. What was so exciting about this practice was that the affirmations were validated through my clients. It reinforced my purpose and gift, which encouraged me to continue moving forward on this path.

There is an energy vibration behind everything in our lives, including how we speak and what we hear. If we use negative words like *hate*, *fear*, *jealousy*, and *doubt*, we will reverberate with lower vibrations of energy and attract similar levels. Alternatively, if we speak words of love, acceptance, and self-worth, our vibration and energy levels will be elevated and attract those similarly high levels. The more we practice reaching an elevated vibration, the easier it will be to recognize our negative thought patterns and flip them around. Our words have the power to inspire and affect real change in this world, but it all starts with us.

DAILY PRACTICE

Self-Discovery through Positive Affirmation

This is both a meditative visualization and a writing exercise, intended to create new positive thought patterns about ourselves through spoken- and written-word affirmations.

Write down a positive, present-tense, loving statement about yourself, even if your first impulse is to doubt it. It helps to use an "I am" statement, such as "I am worthy of love." Think of an affirmation specific to you that represents what you need most. Writing it down gives energy to this thought and brings it into the outer world. Then speak this affirmation aloud throughout your day, which is an important practice that provides energy to the statement. Even if it's just in your car on your way to work, verbalize your statement regularly. There is power in spoken words, like in written words, to transfer thoughts and intentions from the inner world to the outer world.

Once you've written a positive affirmation, use this statement in the following visualization practice.

Focus on your breath to get into a relaxed state. Find comfort in the sanctuary of your inner world. Keep going deeper into yourself. With each breath, let the outer world and all its worries and concerns fade away. Connect with your higher, all-knowing self. Imagine you are surrounded by trees in an enchanted forest at night. In the depths of the forest, a person is standing between the trees among a flurry of fireflies. The person seems familiar, even though you can't quite make out who it is. This draws you in, and as you get closer to the person, you notice they are surrounded by a bright white energy source swirling and flowing, like liquid light in motion.

The vibration of this person resonates at your frequency, and you realize that the light swirling around the person is not fireflies but sparks of electricity in the air. The intensity of your connection grows stronger, and you get so close you feel the sparks lightly brush against you, which is the person's aura flickering around them. You sense they are aware of your presence. Suddenly, the person shifts to look at you. As they do, you realize this person is you. It's your spirit self.

You feel immense, unconditional love as your heart chakra floods with a magical pink light. It's as if this person has always been here waiting for you. Feel the warm light of your spirit self emanating toward you, which grows brighter and more powerful as it charges you. Feel yourself blend with the light and become one with it. Now say your loving affirmation about yourself. As you do, the light becomes more brilliant and expansive. Imagine this light growing so bright that you no longer see anything else. Feel the power of attraction that is within you. This is your light, always within you, always accessible.

When you're ready, open your eyes and return to the room.

Again, say your affirmation out loud. After doing so, notice how you feel lighter, expansive, and powerful. Use this practice to keep your vibration elevated and your words equally so, especially in times when you feel disconnected from your inner source energy — your higher self.

Chapter 6

THE UNIVERSE WITHIN

*Our consciousness must be trained
to dwell on the immortal part in us —
that is the only way to conquer the afflictions of this mortal life.*

— SWAMI PARAMANANDA

Our time in this life is fleeting. We shouldn't waste a moment on unhappiness. There's no need to suffer endlessly. Many people don't realize we all have access to an unlimited, eternal energy source within — Spirit. This energy of the Universe permeates everything and is woven into the fabric of all of us. Some call this supreme energy force God. Others call it a higher power or envision it as many gods. Whatever you call it, it is part of you; it always has been and always will be. When we are disconnected from it and only reliant on our own understanding of why things happen to us, we can feel fragmented, unfocused, and isolated, especially in times of despair. But when we acknowledge Spirit's energy within us and allow ourselves to let go, surrender, and believe in something larger than ourselves, an incredible shift happens on a soul-to-mind level. This force is boundless, untethered by space and time. By understanding our access to this limitlessness, we can move forward in all our actions more confidently, knowing that we have unlimited support from the other side. With that assistance and hope, we are motivated to flourish in every way possible during our relatively short time here on earth.

We are put on this earth for a purpose. Many people spend much of their lives searching for this purpose, seeking external validation, unaware that the answers they seek are already available within them. It may take time to unravel this greater purpose, and that's okay. It's part of our journey. Through meditative practice, we delve deeply into our inner world by letting go, forgiving others, flipping negative thoughts into positive ones, and recognizing how our words affect ourselves and others. When we do these things, we realize a powerful energy that can shape our world. This process brings us closer to our higher power and ultimately affects what we attract to us. I look forward to these practices in my daily life, like stepping into a magical world that heightens my self-awareness. I think of it like the portal to another world in C. S. Lewis's book *The Lion, the Witch, and the Wardrobe.* This is what meditative practice can do — allow us to enter another realm within. There's a level of excitement to this, almost childlike in its ability to transport us into another space.

Most people notice the presence of their higher power during their most difficult moments, such as the death of a loved one, illness, divorce, or the loss of a job. When something bad happens to us, we can feel like we can't move forward, and we can doubt our abilities and strength. These are normal human reactions, but they are responses of the earthly ego. We are all imperfectly perfect as we dance between our human tendencies and higher self-awareness. But if we stay connected to our higher power, we can overcome these difficulties.

When we are faced with self-doubt and the chaos of the outside world, we must remember to return within. If we can find a moment of stillness, we can access the unlimited energy source of Spirit. This is our gateway to peace. I think of it like an hourglass. One side is the external world, and the narrow part is the stillness we must pass through to reach that other side where boundless energy exists. There is an intuitive knowing within that provides patience and understanding that everything will be okay and that what we seek will come to us at the right time. When we practice going within, we engage that knowing.

Everyone's version of success and purpose is different, yet all are equally significant. If we are looking for that purpose and not finding it, it's likely because we are searching outside of ourselves. But the answers are not outside of us. They're locked up in our inner vault, waiting to be discovered. The key to unlocking this is to go within, quiet the mind, and spend time getting to know our spirit self — our higher self. When we do this, we're building our own guidance system as we connect with our spiritual network on the other side, when we put aside the busy schedules and demands we impose upon ourselves. The concepts and practices I've discussed — connecting to source energy, finding strength through meditation, and asking for protection and guidance from spiritual guides on the other side — have served me well as a psychic medium. But the access to this source energy is available to everyone and is the key to gaining greater insight into our life purpose.

When I first realized my gift as a psychic medium, I

resisted it, unaware at the time that it was my greater life purpose. How could something like this be happening to me? And why would I *want* it to happen to me? I thought, *People will think I'm crazy!* But when I acknowledged what was happening in my head, cleared out the negative programming, and trusted my higher power, I made room for the energy to flow through me. I then could delve deeper into my purpose.

One night, many years ago, I was visiting a friend in the countryside. We were around a firepit and talking deeply about life, death, and spirituality. We had just finished doing what I like to call "woo-woo work," which is any kind of ceremonial practice that one does to connect with their higher self and release the things that no longer serve them. When we practice this kind of self-care, we feel a lightness within. It uplifts us and it inspires us to connect with others in a more meaningful way. It was a clear night, and something within me was overcome by the expanse of stars in the sky. In that moment, I realized the vastness of our Universe and felt an infinite feeling within me. On an intuitive level, I realized I reflected that vastness. I could see it within me on an atomic level. I understood that I had a place in all of it and was one with it. When I gave myself to that thought process and belief system, I no longer felt like anything was forced. I didn't fight it. I had enormous energy available, and I surrendered to that force. As I let people come to me and as the elements of my gift became more evident, I realized there was a greater purpose for my life. I was a messenger.

After the epiphany I had under the stars — I was in the early stages of exploring my newfound gift — other psychic mediums told me they saw my gift reaching heights that would attract people to me globally. Let me tell you, for a private person who was trying to figure out my purpose, that was frightening. But I reminded myself that fear dims our light and disconnects us from source energy, and the only way out is within.

I practiced my connection with Spirit by putting forth the intention to bring people to me who needed healing through my gift. That was precisely what happened — and quickly. Embracing this side of me led me down a path that brought me into contact with some incredible people doing selfless work for the greater good of others. This is how you know you're on the right path in life — when you attract the right kind of people into your orbit.

I began doing private readings for individuals, and by word of mouth, my clientele grew exponentially. With momentum building, I felt compelled to channel messages to larger groups of people in audience settings. I held a few audience readings, which were modestly attended, but it wasn't until I was presented with the opportunity to channel for a charity event for the Leukemia & Lymphoma Society that things took off. Soon after that, various venues called, and hundreds of people attended each one. The healing at these events was far beyond anything I could have dreamed. Before long, national media sought me for interviews, my Facebook following grew to more than two hundred thousand, my waiting list for private readings grew to more than two years, and multiple publishers were interested in my story becoming a book. My success is a testament to trusting in Spirit, surrendering, and taking time for inner work. This is what led me to where I was supposed to be.

People often seek external gratification or validation from others or attempt to fill themselves with the material world, but none of this brings everlasting fulfillment. We cannot take these things to the afterlife. Happiness is only found within us. Finding what matters is a soul exploration. This is where our two sides, the earthly ego and the spirit self, meet. That connection is what leads me where I know I am meant to go. I continually stay connected to my higher power throughout the journey of life, and I trust that every twist I encounter along the road is part of my greater purpose. Anytime I feel over-whelmed, I meditate to recenter myself, letting go of anything that doesn't serve me well.

Because we are in the flesh, we're always going to be part of this dance between the human and spiritual sides of our exis-tence. It's up to us to find the right balance to create the world we desire and to flourish. We know there's an imbalance be-tween these two sides if we feel stuck or at a low vibration. But when we recognize the infinite energy source within working on our behalf for our greatest good, waiting for us to answer the call by engaging with it, that flow of energy and the excite-ment it produces burst into life. That's when we know we have attained the balance we need to live our best life.

DAILY PRACTICE

Discovering Your Own Universe Within

This visualization meditation helps you to explore your vast inner world and recognize how your potential manifests from the perva-sive energy throughout the Universe.

For this meditation, it's best to have a visual of the stars in the Universe. This implants the Universe's vastness in your mind's eye. That could mean going outside under the night sky and taking in the scenery, or finding a vivid photo of galaxies or clusters of stars, and spend a few moments immersed in this imagery. You also may want to put on some soothing ethereal music in the background.

Take a deep breath and exhale. Repeat this several times until you are in a relaxed state. Visualize yourself floating comfortably among the stars in the Milky Way galaxy. Feel the expansive space beneath you and in all directions. Notice stars appear like tiny pinpoints in the distance. Take in the beauty of this vast expanse as you float in space. Here, you can reach the edges of the galaxy in the blink of an eye. This is the power your mind has to carry you anywhere you choose. There is infinite energy in this place as stars are born all around you. This is life in the making.

As you float in the empty space of the galaxy, feel pulled toward the pinpoints of starlight in the distance. Don't resist this pull. Let this natural process take you where you are supposed to go. There's nothing for you to do except be. No worries or fears; only pure presence. As you are pulled toward the milky-white lights of these star clusters, their glow grows brighter, and you are received in a loving embrace by sunbeams. Bask in the warmth of this loving light for as long as you need. You are one with the light. There is no separation. The light will always be part of you, accessible whenever you need it. Sense the light all around as its warmth carries you deeper into yourself.

Now the space around you narrows into a funnel that carries you into another realm. Find the stillness within as you transition from one realm to the next. Within this narrowing, there is a vortex of light ahead, and you know that you can take only your light through. You must leave your physical self behind, but you can return to your physical self whenever you please. This is your personal passageway. Notice how easily you glide deeper into this comforting feeling. Surrender to the power of this energy as it draws you in. This vortex of light is effortless. The Universe no longer feels external. It is you, and you are it. This is your energy source.

Pass through the neck of the hourglass. You are no longer among the stars but rather among blueish-white pinpoints of light all around. You are in the inner world now, the realm of possibility. Those points of light are the tiniest structures in the Universe, small particles bouncing about and twirling, vibrating in all directions. They work effortlessly to manifest into existence. This vast space inside you is home, where everything is born. These tiny particles make up all that is you. This is your place for self-discovery. There's an excitement here, with a warm, comforting energy moving about. Intentions are born in this realm of possibilities. Spend some time in this inner place. Ask your higher self what your greater purpose is in this life. Listen to the inner voice unabridged, unfiltered.

When you are ready, open your eyes and return to the physical world.

Take a moment to journal about your experience. What has this connection to the limitless power source within taught you? What is the most significant takeaway from your inner journey? Return to this place often. It will strengthen each time.

Chapter 7

THE GRATITUDE
FREQUENCY

*This moment of gratitude is a moment of enlightenment,
of mindfulness, of intelligence. It is a manifestation
from the depths of your consciousness.*

— THICH NHAT HANH

The wise Buddhist monk Thich Nhat Hanh often spoke about the magic in simple moments of gratitude that manifest from within to bring about joy. This is a reminder that the path to true happiness is paved in gratitude.

With gratitude in your heart, abundance will come in all aspects of your life. You will see the extraordinary in the ordinary. With a conscious acknowledgment of gratitude, life becomes more vibrant and vivid, even in the most ordinary tasks. Gratitude is like turning the dial on a handheld radio: The more we turn it, the better chance we have of picking up the right frequency. Every time we express gratitude for something, we tune in to Spirit at a higher vibration, where anything is possible. Spirit encourages us to plug in to the here and now through this open frequency channel to experience our version of heaven on earth. Heaven on earth doesn't mean having it all; it means having an appreciation for what we *do* have. It means taking advantage of those small moments that bring the most joy, like watching a sunrise, sipping morning coffee, eating a favorite meal, connecting with family, or creating art. These are moments money can't buy.

When we live with appreciation for what we have, and do so continually with presence and gratitude, we reinforce positive thoughts and attraction. Gratitude is an extension of the practice of flipping the negative thoughts of ego into positive higher-self thoughts. Every moment we give gratitude, we promote more positive thoughts to grow within us. Gratitude rewires the mind and allows us to think more openly and positively, building the foundation for a new belief system about ourselves. Spirit can easily connect with us when we are in this heightened state of awareness because we are detached from our ego and aligned with the energy on the other side.

To make gratitude part of who we are requires our conscious attention throughout each day. Eventually, it becomes routine, and we naturally gravitate toward grateful thoughts. It doesn't take enormous effort to see the results, but it does take introspection. We must recognize a lack-mind state, which is when we are consumed with thoughts of wishing for what we don't have, like a bigger house, a slimmer body, a nicer car, or more well-behaved kids. Yes, we should flip those negatives into positives, but we can go even deeper. Be truthful about what you are grateful for in your life. What do you have to lose?

For example, when I moved back to Southern California in 2009 after college, life was much different. I worried whether I had made the right decision leaving my identity as an opera singer behind. Despite these doubts, the pull I felt toward helping people in need had grown stronger. This ability within me to connect to the other side could not be denied. I had to put an unbreakable trust in Spirit and move forward with sharing my gift as a channel for others. I had to cast aside my fears and doubts about *if* I could succeed — and just trust that I would.

Many people face similar fears after college, but I had to dive deeper into trust by building a strong confidence in myself as a bridge between our world and the realm of Spirit. It doesn't matter what your gift is; the courage to pursue what you are destined for comes from faith in something greater. During that time in my life, I learned what powerful tools surrendering and giving gratitude could be. Every morning, I thanked God for each new day, my family, my friends, and my health. I gave gratitude for all the little things, like the warm water in the shower, a roof over my head on a cold morning, heat from the furnace, the meal I was about to eat, and a car that allowed me to reach the places I needed to go. The more I expressed gratitude, the easier it was to see what I should be grateful for. When I got a text from someone, I gave gratitude for living in a world with cell phones that keep me connected to loved ones. The more I spent time in these thoughts, the more grateful I became.

This new mindset I was developing complemented my connection to Spirit and my psychic self, deepening my understanding of how the other side works. I started to use gratitude as a tool to raise my vibration to new levels. Through repeated expressions of gratitude, I reached a place where I could mentally blend with Spirit naturally. This works so well because Spirit exists in a heightened state of perpetual love

and gratitude for all that is. After experiencing how this connection between gratitude and Spirit works, I was excited to
give gratitude throughout my day. I soon noticed all my earthly
needs being met beautifully while I focused on my mission of
serving others as a channel for Spirit.

I was still working on my self-worth at the time, only
charging a nominal fee for my readings. I continued, all the
same, to thank Spirit for inspiring others to spread the word
about my gift. I gave gratitude to my mom on the other side
for giving me life and guiding me along the path that allowed
me to succeed and prosper. Within months, I had a client
named Michelle, who invited me to her home in Lake Forest
for her first-ever reading. On the drive to her house, I focused
on my gratitude. Her neighborhood was nestled in a beautiful
natural setting with tall trees. I gave gratitude for the beauty
of this environment. I felt a sense of overwhelming calmness
when I arrived at her house.

The reading was powerful and so affirming to her. The undeniable validations she received proved to her that we do go
on after death, that we are eternal. She still talks with gratitude
in her heart about the experience she had with me and how
it profoundly and forever changed her. When I finished the
reading, she walked me to my car. Her face was beaming with
a bright smile. She said, "I want to give you what I feel you
deserve for this experience," and she gave me more than twice
the amount I was charging at the time. This was when I realized how interwoven gratitude and manifestation could be. It
ultimately leads us to greater abundance and higher self-worth
because they vibrate at the same frequency.

When you live in a state of gratitude, you're aligned with
Spirit. You're elevating your vibration because you see life in a

better way. You detach from the chaos of a situation and recognize the love and manifestation of God around you. When you're in this elevated mental space, you're more resilient to life's challenges, and it's more difficult for anybody or anything to knock you down. It doesn't mean everything will always go right, but when something doesn't go right, you will see it in the best light possible, which makes overcoming those obstacles much more manageable.

Yes, awful experiences, such as the death of a loved one, still happen. In moments like these, expressing gratitude for anything may be the furthest thing from our minds. But we *can* give gratitude for the memories and the love we shared. The only thing we can control is our attitude. In his book *Man's Search for Meaning*, Viktor Frankl wrote about the atrocities he and others faced in Nazi death camps during World War II. He said, "Everything can be taken from a man but one thing: the last of the human freedoms — to choose one's attitude in any given set of circumstances, to choose one's own way." Even in the face of the worst atrocities, we still have the power to choose our thoughts, to choose gratitude. These are some of life's most important moments — when we need to let go and allow grief to flow through us so we can process what is happening and not allow it to hold us back as we try to move forward. Grief is painful, especially when a loved one dies, but grief is actually an accumulation of all the love we've stored within for that person. So, ultimately, grief is the release of love. As we process grief and eventually give gratitude for that person and their presence and influence in our lives, we can swing that pendulum to a positive place.

I encourage you to focus on the simple mantra "thank you." Repeat this throughout the day to reinforce gratitude for everything. I try to say thank you as many times a day as possible — at home, in the car, in line at the grocery store. I give gratitude for the ability to pause in the moment and live presently. I consider each gratitude mantra like adding money to a magical piggy bank. Remember how exciting and satisfying it was to fill up a piggy bank as a child and hear that clink as the change dropped in? Gratitude has the same effect. It's like filling a bank with gratitude coins. Each coin is charged with energy for our spiritual health, and the bank glows with golden light with each deposit.

For me, the "savings" payoff occurs when my mind wanders or worries, and I'm struggling to let go of something. That's when I can go to my gratitude piggy bank and crack it open. This creates an aura of abundance, helping me recognize that I have everything I already need — and that I am exactly where I need to be. As I reap the riches of this accumulation of positive energy, I can refocus on what matters and realign my overall intention of peace and joy. I remind myself of my purpose and the support I have from Spirit. I then imagine this magical piggy bank is whole again, waiting to repeat the process, so I may continue to replenish it with my gratitude savings.

Giving gratitude disconnects us from our earthly ego, preventing this side of us from running our lives. Saying "thank you" breaks that ego cycle and plugs us back into that strong, palpable feeling of the heartbeat of the Universe.

DAILY PRACTICE

The Gratitude Bank

This visualization exercise helps you build an inner dialogue of gratitude, take stock of what you are grateful for, and shift your inner narrative from a mindset of lack to one of abundance.

Do this practice daily for three weeks to give it ample time to become a natural part of your routine. You probably won't even want to stop once you see how positive you feel. Practice this each night before bed, just before sleep, so it has a chance to sink deeply into your subconscious. Repeat this each morning as soon as you wake up, setting your alarm five minutes early, if necessary. The imagery you focus on will assist you in reinforcing grateful thoughts throughout the day.

Practice some deep natural breathing to get yourself into a relaxed and calm space. Close your eyes and visualize a gold piggy bank, like the simple kind children use. In your mind's eye, see it, touch it, and connect with it. Now fill your piggy bank with those things you are most grateful for. Visualize a coin of pure golden light, and infuse your gratitude into this energetically charged coin. Start with the simple phrase "thank you." Feel the warmth from this transformative expression blend effortlessly with the coin of light. Every time you say "thank you," you give grace to the world around you and the entirety of the Universe. Imagine the coin of light entering the slot and illuminating the piggy bank from the inside out. Repeat this for as many things you feel grateful for as possible. There is no limit to the number of coins — whatever feels right. With each deposit, visualize the piggy bank glowing brighter and brighter.

The more gratitude statements you make, the more the golden light flows from the top of the piggy bank and reaches the darkest crevices in your mind. This light fills you up, causing a shift to happen within — a more positive vibration.

As the days go on, you will start to feel the effects of this light filling you up throughout the day. It's an enormous payoff for a small amount of time. You'll feel more confident, grounded, connected, and abundant in all ways.

Chapter 8

PRAYING IT FORWARD

God speaks in the silence of the heart.
Listening is the beginning of prayer.

— ST. TERESA OF CALCUTTA

Prayer is a process of active dialogue with our higher power throughout our journey on earth. It's a sacred connection to the invisible realm of Spirit, one in which there is a trust that "someone" is listening who will unburden us, support us, and guide us where we need to be. Prayer opens our eyes to how we can be of service to others and pay it forward by being the answer to someone else's prayer.

When I call it "active dialogue," I mean prayer is a conversation we can have daily, even multiple times a day. The more we pray, the more connected we become to this sacred relationship and our understanding of our purpose in life. Prayer is a form of giving gratitude and surrendering. Even someone who has never been spiritually active or taught how to pray has something within their soul intuitively telling them there is something bigger. The question is whether they will choose to listen to and act upon that intuition by taking a leap of faith into the unknown.

Prayer can lead to extraordinary acts in the most ordinary moments, and this has ripple effects on the world around us. A friend of mine, Anthony, told me about an experience in a grocery store where he experienced just that. He was in a hurry and planned to use the self-checkout lane, but when he got to that line, he noticed a nun in the line next to him; a cashier was scanning her groceries. Anthony was taught by nuns in elementary school and had a tremendous amount of respect for their calling of service to others. He wanted to get home quickly, but as someone who prays each day, his active dialogue called upon him to act differently than planned. He felt pulled, intuitively, to the nun's line.

Anthony followed his gut instinct and got into line behind the nun. An elderly gentleman then got in line behind him. As the cashier — a young man barely beyond his teen years — continued to scan the nun's groceries, Anthony pulled out his credit card and told the nun he would pay for them. She was stunned and appreciative — but that was just the start.

After Anthony paid for her groceries, the elderly man behind him, who witnessed this act of kindness, handed a twenty-dollar bill to the nun to use as she needed. Anthony and the gentleman then struck up a friendly conversation. This act, inspired by prayer, was a catalyst for a human connection in what could have been just a routine stop at the store. Every moment in the presence of other people is an opportunity for human connection and acts of generosity. This brings us closer to the divine, which is the intention Spirit has for our lives. While

this was all happening, the young cashier watched in amaze-
ment, appreciating the love and charity between these strang-
ers. All of this transpired spontaneously because of Anthony's
connection to his higher power through prayer.

You may say, "I don't need to pray to feel inspired to do good
for others." This is true, and many atheists have strong moral
compasses, but Anthony's inspiration from his connection to
prayer is proof that prayer is a form of positive thought reinforcement, intention-setting, and surrender, which can lead to
acts of kindness. If Anthony hadn't been connected to a higher
power, it might never have occurred to him to do what he did.
Because prayer reinforces positive thought patterns, it can lead
to positive actions that someone not connected to prayer may
not recognize as easily. And paying it forward doesn't have
to be a physical act. Whenever someone is in need, prayer in
and of itself can be a loving act for another. I often surround
someone with a blanket of white healing light. Prayer may be
as simple as that — asking Spirit to envelop another with a
loving embrace.

Prayer opens our eyes to opportunities all around us to pay
it forward, which can be inspiring. Like the man in line behind Anthony, when someone witnesses someone else pay it
forward, they want to do the same. Giving twenty dollars to
the nun may seem random, but the gentleman felt compelled
to do *something* after watching Anthony's actions. There is also
the strong possibility these acts affected the young cashier, a
witness to all of this kindness. Good deeds tend to have a but-
terfly effect, as one action leads to many more.

I encourage you to pray for an opportunity to help somebody in need, as this is one of the greatest gifts we can give to
another. The act of giving not only elevates the other person

but lifts *you* up as well. In divine time, your prayer will be answered, and you will be presented with the chance to be the miracle in someone else's life. This is your opportunity to be a vessel for Spirit to shine through you, to be an answer to somebody else's prayer.

When I think of the healing power of prayer and acts of kindness, I think of my good friend Michelle (whom I introduce in chapter 7). Michelle lives her life through acts of kindness. She's also a successful businesswoman with a vast knowledge of entrepreneurship.

Michelle loves to travel, and she often travels to Laos, a country between Vietnam and Thailand. On one trip with her friend Julie, they had breakfast each day at a hotel café perched above the Mekong River. Here they met a server named Sithong, who was forever changed by their chance encounter. As one of the few servers who spoke English, Sithong immediately connected with Michelle and Julie. Every day, Michelle and Julie asked Sithong questions about Luang Prabang, the town they were visiting. In particular, they wanted to know more about the monks who strolled the quaint streets. Sithong was delighted to chat with them. He explained that he had been a Buddhist monk for eight years, but he had left the monkhood at eighteen because he dreamed of going to college and starting his own business one day. Since he made only fifty cents an hour at the café, it was going to take him a long time to save for college.

Sithong offered to take Michelle and Julie to the temples after work and be their tour guide. They were thrilled, and Sithong took them to the main temple, where he was once a monk. At five o'clock each afternoon, the monks gathered in a building to pray and chant. Sithong led the ladies into the back of the temple and told them it was okay to record and take photos. Michelle and Julie were grateful for such an incredible opportunity. They would never have been permitted to do this without him.

On two more afternoons, Sithong took Michelle and Julie on area tours and shared stories of his upbringing in a remote little village, five hours away from Luang Prabang. He was one of seven children, the youngest and only one to graduate from high school. His dream was to further his education and help support his poor family. On their last night in Luang Prabang, Michelle and Julie withdrew money from every ATM in town, since each had a daily limit on funds. Between them, they collected fifteen hundred dollars, which was enough for a year of tuition at the local college.

In the morning, Sithong came to say goodbye as Michelle and Julie were getting ready to head to the airport, and they handed him an envelope on which they had written, "We believe in you." With tears in her eyes, Michelle said, "You need to follow your dreams, and we want to help you do it." Sithong was taken aback by the unbelievable kindness of these two women, but they weren't finished. They made him an offer: If he continued to go to school, they would continue to help him. Of course, he agreed, and Michelle and Julie made return trips to Laos over the next three years, giving Sithong more money each time until he finally graduated.

After graduation, Sithong found work at another café, but it paid only seventy cents an hour, which was still not a livable wage. Michelle and Julie suggested he ask for a dollar an hour, but the café owners declined. Undeterred, the ladies saw this hurdle as a blessing in disguise for Sithong. While shopping at the local night market, they noticed there were no T-shirt souvenirs to take home to friends and family. So they suggested that Sithong start a business selling T-shirts. Michelle's son, an illustrator, offered to create some beautiful designs, and Sithong found a local silk screener and blank T-shirts for printing. Michelle and Julie also taught him to make necklaces with antique Buddhist amulets to sell, and they provided the funds for fifty necklaces and four hundred shirts. After three months of running this business, Sithong had saved over ten thousand US dollars, and he eventually quit his café job and rented a shop. Today, proceeds from this business help support a dormitory for girls from the countryside, where there are no schools, so that they can receive an education in Luang Prabang.

I love this story because it's a testament to how a good deed can inspire others to do the same in profound and unforeseen ways. It's a reminder that we all have an opportunity to answer somebody else's prayer if we listen to our inner voice, that active dialogue within ourselves. Michelle and Julie "prayed" it forward when an opportunity presented itself. By helping Sithong find a way out of poverty, they not only gave him the nuts and bolts to build a new life, but they inspired him to do the same for others. He told them, "I want to do the kindness." This is what it means to pray it forward. He helped others continue their education, which is a step toward ending poverty in those families as well.

Michelle is a living example of what it means to be called to action. In the same way that she saw my potential and worth when I read for her so many years ago, she saw potential in Sithong and helped him. We all have an opportunity to be a prayer in action, to be a vessel for Spirit's manifestation of love in this world — should we choose to answer the call.

DAILY PRACTICE

Prayers for Empowerment and Transformation

Recite these and other prayers to engage in an active dialogue with Spirit, build trust with your higher power, and move toward your greater purpose in life while being in service to others.

Prayer is a powerful tool that we can use anytime to realign with our higher self — our all-knowing self. This is our deep connection to our faith. With daily repetition, we can navigate ourselves back to peace, flow, and the universal energy of pure and unconditional love. It's an act of ultimate trust and surrender to the creator of all that is. To further develop this foundation of trust, I enjoy starting my day with this process of prayer.

Create a sacred space, a sanctuary for this dialogue with your higher power, even if it's just a corner of a room where you can light a candle. This sacred space should reflect your inner self. To recite prayers or mantras, I also like to use a mala. This is a string of beads in which each bead represents a mantra. A mala is similar to a Catholic rosary, in which each bead represents a Christian prayer, and you can use a rosary if you wish. Find what feels right for you to make this connection with ease.

I suggest doing this practice in the morning before the buzzing energy of the day interferes. Then you can take this dialogue with you throughout the day. Whenever you feel you need to refresh, recall how you felt while praying and make that divine connection. Below are three prayers you can use, though you can also develop your own. Make this practice a daily ritual, and let inspiration and your intuition guide you to adapt it as you wish.

Prayer No. 1: The Divine Guidance

Dear Spirit,
Thank you for my life.
For all the blessings I see and haven't recognized yet.
For this new day on earth in the flesh.
Thank you for being my guide.
Thank you for the love.
I call upon all spiritual allies to surround me in a white
    light of protection from all harm.
I ask that you help me see all things through my innate
    spiritual lens so I may learn and grow.
Please show me the way to peace.
Shine through me so that I may be a beacon of love to
    each person I encounter in my day.
I surrender all earthly concerns to you and trust that
    everything is working out for my highest good.
I allow your divine love to guide me.
I surrender to thy will, and so it will be done.

Prayer No. 2: An Eternal Trust

Dear God,
Today, I trust that I am an answer to someone's prayer.
Today, I trust that someone will be an answer to my
    prayer.
Always, I trust in an infinite life everlasting.
Always, I trust that you will guide me and protect me on
    my journey.

Prayer No. 3: In Service to Others

Dear Universe (the Creator of all that Is),
Please show me the way to acceptance.

Please show me the way to surrender.

Please show me how to be of service to those in need.

Please show me how to serve my purpose.

Please show me the way to shine your light upon others.

You are the infinite light that never leaves.

We are never separate.

Chapter 9

LOVING LIFE'S CHALLENGES

If you believe it will work out, you'll see opportunities.
If you believe it won't, you will see obstacles.

— WAYNE DYER

Our most difficult challenges can also be our greatest turning points, each a crossroads where we have to decide how to move forward. These moments can bring a pivotal shift in our perceptions, a change in how we view our world, and most significantly, opportunities for personal growth. Inner growth comes from how we meet the challenge, and our attitude toward each challenge defines us. When someone we love dies, if we get sick with a serious disease, when a pandemic grips our world, if our country breaks out in war — these significant challenges, some personal, some global, can be turning points that lead to opportunities for positive change within and around us.

The deeper we get into a challenge, the more important it

is to flip our thinking about it. We need to let go of what no longer serves us, find inner strength, give gratitude for what we have, and seize opportunities to do good. This is how we keep our vibration elevated in a positive place. We live our best life when we face challenges, persevere, and survive. This is the space from which personal growth is built. Turning back out of fear after our world is blown wide open is a missed opportunity and takes us nowhere. We are born out of the realm of Spirit, brought into life to learn lessons and gain new perspectives on a soul level, so we can grow and learn to appreciate the gift of making loving connections with each other.

I believe we are all born into this life with a plan rooted in love and mapped out for us by our higher power. But because we have free will and our actions affect one another, we often encounter speed bumps and obstacles along our path that we need strength to move past. Those challenges remind us of what is important, where we should be directing our energy, and how blessed we are no matter our situation. The challenges we encounter reconnect us to that love from our initial plan, like a soul recognition of our greater purpose. With that reconnection, we can survive anything and even one day thrive again, no matter how complex or even tragic a challenge becomes.

We all continue to face one of the biggest challenges of our generation: the Covid-19 pandemic. Initially, the virus caused widespread fear as people across the globe became sick and often died. Fear defined daily life as people isolated, stopped traveling, attended school virtually, and sometimes lost their jobs. People were afraid to go to the store, shake hands, hug, or even be near others. To varying degrees, this continues today. We remain challenged with how to stay connected with loved ones while remaining safe from the virus — a reminder of how important it is to have human connection. Of course, many people and companies have risen to the challenge in numerous ways: We now possess multiple effective vaccines, we have learned the best protocols to keep people virus-free, and working from home is becoming accepted. Some challenges have been more difficult than others to overcome, and some of the solutions — like in-home learning for schoolchildren — have presented challenges in themselves.

The pandemic has forced people and societies to "pivot" in order to meet challenges together and help each other survive. Worldwide, people have shown some extraordinary acts of kindness. And over time, as we learn to live with the virus, people's fears have lessened, and we've focused not only on surviving, but on persevering and coming through stronger than before. Despite the continuing challenges of the virus, we have a new appreciation for things we may have taken for granted before, such as a simple handshake, hug, or visit with grandparents. We have a newfound appreciation for all of our relationships — family and friends, coworkers and acquaintances — because we now realize that our greatest gift in life is each other. Life is fragile, and we've learned how much we rely on each other, so we must nurture all relationships with care and respect. The pandemic has been a global call to action, and many have listened and helped people who were struggling and been the answer to someone else's prayer.

Remember our nasty little companion, the earthly ego? This is where our fear dwells. The ego often regards challenges like impassable roadblocks. It responds to obstacles with despair rather than embracing them as opportunities. Yes, some obstacles block our way, but we can still succeed by "pivoting" and finding or creating new ways to reach our goals. This is rarely easy; quite the contrary. But the harder the challenge, the greater the reward when we overcome it. Accepting a challenge also involves risk: Our solution might fail, but it might not. What's most important is never losing faith in ourselves to face whatever challenges arise, and to operate each day with love for ourselves and others. Challenges aren't a curse or a failure, but sometimes they are an opportunity to go in a new direction.

Sithong's story is a good example (see pages 72–74). After leaving the monastery in Laos, he could easily have given up on his life goals and become miserable, since his café job didn't pay enough for him to succeed. Yet his positive attitude, and his continuing decision to take a risk on himself, is why he inspired Michelle and Julie to help him. Sithong manifested abundance in a way he could not have foreseen. Challenges are merely part of our overall journey, like a long hike through a mountainous region. There will be peaks and valleys, sunshine and darkness, smooth terrain and dangerous obstacles, times when we can see the road ahead and times when we cannot. But no matter what challenges arise, our love for the journey enables us to approach difficulties with confidence, to find value in them and keep moving forward, stronger than before.

Challenges aren't always earth-shattering, but even smaller challenges can profoundly affect us. When I was younger, I struggled with my relationship with food. Too much of it, specifically. When I look back, I realize how much I struggled. I'm sure a big reason was that, at times, my meals were inconsistent, especially while I lived in New York with my mom as a kid; I didn't always know when my next meal would come. I can recall a time when my mom pulled out frozen peaches for my meal. That was all we had. So, when I had the opportunity to eat a real meal, I took advantage of it and binged on junk. I found comfort in food, almost instinctually from a survival standpoint, never knowing when my next chance to eat would be.

When I lived with my grandma in California, she fed me a lot because this was how she showed her love, but it was usually some sort of fast food, not the healthiest choices. "You're a growing boy," she said as I continued to pack on the pounds. I think this was her way of ensuring that I never went hungry again. At the same time, I had a lack mentality with food. I felt like I needed to get as much of it as possible because of my subconscious fear. That continued throughout high school and college. What I didn't fully grasp at the time was how food was particularly grounding for me as an empathic person, which is why I found so much comfort in it. Intuitive or empathic people live in a state of heightened interconnectedness with others, which can be draining. So, many empathic people find comfort in earthly pleasures because they bring us back to earth. This can be quite a challenge if we don't know how to control it. We must be aware of balancing mind, body, and spirit to live with more vitality. When our vessel — the body — is clear, we can expand our spiritual gifts more wholly.

In my early twenties, I noticed my weight was holding me down, literally and figuratively. At Chinese restaurants, I would eat everything on the plate, even if I was full, and it would make me sick. I knew I had to do something for the good of my health. My relationship with food had become toxic. I welcomed the challenge of losing weight, embracing exercise, and changing my habits because I did not want to be that person anymore. I wanted to feel good about myself, and I knew that the path to my happiness required pushing through the difficulty of the task. I wanted to be stronger emotionally, physically, and spiritually. I knew this was an opportunity for personal growth.

I changed by learning to give gratitude for what I had and making different choices, like saving half of my food for later so that nothing went to waste. I stopped feeling like I had to eat everything because it was in front of me. Slowly but surely, I changed my relationship with food. On one particular day, as I walked down the street after a meal out, I saw a homeless man and gave him my leftovers. I was changing how my mind worked, reminding myself that I didn't need to worry about the next meal. There would be enough for me and enough to share with someone in need.

I eventually found comfort in physical activity rather than in food. When I viewed the challenge as something that could better me, it uplifted me in every aspect of my life. I fell in love with how physical activity made me feel. I felt euphoric by pushing myself with exercise rather than indulging in food. I learned the power of shifting my mental state and trusting my body to heal itself and transform. I was "flipping those negatives," as I like to say. I never would have succeeded without positive self-talk for motivation. It also helped to see the results of my efforts each week, which motivated me to keep going. Breaking down challenges into small goals makes any challenge much more attainable. Since then, I've also been able to keep off all the weight I lost.

Yes, this takes daily dedication, but I've learned it's important to continually take care of the body, mind, and spirit. All three are part of the whole and must be cared for regularly, which is why I make meditation and physical activity part of my routine. Not only is physical activity my "go-to" for grounding, but it simultaneously elevates me energetically. This balanced state can connect us to source energy. I feel focused and "in my body" when exercising. It's similar to the "runner's high," which is that space between our body and mind where endurance and perseverance are born. That meditative state is the same space where we can connect with Spirit.

That said, I still sometimes find it challenging to stay away from foods I know I shouldn't eat and to work out every day, but the habits I've created allow me to overcome such challenges. I've also changed my rituals when it comes to eating meals. I spend a few moments before every meal giving gratitude for the energy exchange that is about to occur. The food we eat is just that — a transformation of energy. Whether a plant or animal, our food was once living, and it deserves gratitude and respect for giving us the energy it has stored within, which allows us to live another day.

There are always two ways of looking at life: with fear, where things happen to us and we can't do anything about them, or through love, where we can shape our world and have an opportunity to grow from the challenges we face. When we live in the vibration of love, we are in an ever-present state of readiness for challenges. It's okay that we don't know what challenges we will face because we are supported by our spiritual network on the other side, and that spiritual network is omnipresent and everlasting. We can live without fear. Whatever challenges us can serve a greater purpose: to help transform us in miraculous ways.

DAILY PRACTICE

Soaring from a Higher Perspective

This visualization meditation focuses on the supporting power of the white light to elevate us so that we can observe our challenges from a higher perspective.

Observing any obstacle or challenge from a higher spiritual perspective lifts the heaviness we feel from any fears of the unknown. Through this visualization practice, you transform the challenges you face into something meaningful. You break through the roadblocks created by your earthly ego that prevent you from moving forward. This allows you to gain a fresh perspective of your situation.

Focus on your challenge, problem, or worry — whatever is heaviest on your heart. Imagine all the elements of this situation, such as the people, setting, and feelings you have about it. Now, take a snapshot of it in your mind.

Next, take a deep breath while visualizing a warm white light entering the top of your head. As you exhale, see the white light filling the space around you. Feel the light enter you from above. With each breath, feel the light filling your lungs. As you exhale, picture the light carrying your worry away into tiny light particles, which disintegrate peacefully into the air. With each exhalation, feel lighter and more elevated. Repeat this as many times as you need to get into a relaxed state. Know that surrendering to the white light is your most potent tool for transformation. Allow yourself to be filled with its loving warmth. See this light glow from your body as it emanates from within.

The ever-expansive light glows brighter and brighter around you, transforming all darkness into a loving light. As the light expands, so do you, ever higher and more elevated as you and the light become one. Give your worries and challenges to the light. They are not your burden to carry alone anymore. Sense this radiant white light energy enveloping you. Let your trust in your intuition grow stronger as the light around you grows brighter. The light elevates you into a higher spiritual plane — a higher perspective. Know that the white light will always be part of you when you face challenges, assisting you in moving forward. It is your protector. This eternal white light is limitless. It is the light of Spirit, the Divine One, the light of God, capable of transforming the darkest of situations into miracles.

Feel the weightlessness from this higher perspective as you float further into the sky above. You can see everything from up here. This is your soul — your higher self — watching the busy world unfold below. Feel the stillness within from this bird's eye view. There's no sound, just perspective. Everything becomes clearer from up here. Now you can see the whole picture. You are limitless from above. You can go anywhere easily, whenever you want. When you're ready to come back down into the room, plant your feet firmly on the ground to anchor you back into your body. You carry the white light within you always. Trust that the white light transforms your challenges into blessings. Know that with the support of the white light to protect and shield you, you can move in and out of any of life's challenging situations with greater ease by looking at it from a fresh perspective.

Chapter 10

THE SPIRITUAL WEB

*Important encounters are planned by the souls
long before the bodies see each other.*
— PAULO COELHO

We each have a spiritual web, layers of energy woven through the very fabric of our being, that guides us from the other side on our earthly journey. This web is a loving, nurturing, energy network that connects us to the spiritual realm. It uplifts and assists us in living our best life possible. The nature of the spiritual web, much like the silk of a spider's web, is meant to support and sustain us. It is woven through us by the very existence of the other side — whose nature is everlasting love. The love in this web is not like earthly ego love, which is conditional, with expectations that must be met and emotional taking. That's ego-minded trickery. This is unconditional love, something we only get a glimpse of in life if we remain open and let it in.

The spiritual web is comprised of three main groups on the other side:

- Spirit guides — once-living souls who directly guide us from the other side.
- Ascended masters — enlightened souls who incarnated into life and profoundly impacted the world when they were here.
- Angels — the highest vibration of energy, beings who have never been in our physical world but continue to guide and protect us from the other side.

This web of spiritual energy guides us on our life's journey. When we open our hearts to it and recognize its influential presence, we can connect to it through prayer and recognize its support in everything we do. If you feel you are going about this life alone, don't be mistaken — you are always supported. It may not feel that way sometimes because the spiritual realm — the "invisible world" where all this support comes from — is not directly seeable. However, if you know how to connect to this vast, supportive spiritual network, you will observe and sense it.

This web always supports us, helping us learn and conquer the daily challenges of life. It has been with us in past lives before we were born into this world, and it will continue to be with us throughout our eternal spiritual journey.

Spirit guides, the first level of energy in the spiritual web, aren't necessarily people we have known in our lives. They could be a relative who died before we were born or someone we lived with in a previous life thousands of years ago. There's no limit to our connections and no distance too far between lifetimes for those souls. Part of their purpose as spiritual guides is to nudge us in the right direction for our greatest spiritual growth.

For example, a spirit guide might present opportunities for an alcoholic to get help, or they might do something to alert a person about a health issue they should get checked. Let's say a woman has been putting off going to the doctor for a routine checkup. Then one day a voice in her head says, *Just get your checkup. Get it over with.* So she goes and the doctor finds a lump in her breast that needs to be removed. Had she waited longer, it might have progressed and been inoperable, but luckily she catches it in time. That "knowing" or voice in her mind to act is a nudge from her spirit guide.

I often receive messages like this about future or recent incidents during client readings. This is how spirit guides help us from the other side. Which spirit guides help us often will depend on their expertise in life. For example, if I had a grandfather who was an alcoholic, he would likely be my spirit guide in protecting me from harm related to addiction. Although guides are in heaven, they are still working for us with respect to what their roles were here on earth. They do what they can to make our lives better until we eventually join them, when it will be our turn to help our living network of souls on earth.

Our second level of energy in the spiritual web is the ascended masters. Ascended masters are much like spirit guides, but they are accomplished, well-known figures with insights about spiritual connections that most people don't have. Examples of ascended masters are Abraham, Buddha, Jesus Christ, and Gandhi — just to name of few of the countless others who have contributed to elevating human consciousness over the centuries. Like spirit guides, they have a mission to enlighten us, to help us change and become better people, though they work on a broader scale in moving humanity in new directions of enlightenment. The ascended masters present themselves when we go through our greatest spiritual evolution — our awakening — either through curiosity or complete and utter surrender. Often, when we have reached the end of our rope, when we face challenges we think we can't handle alone, these masters of enlightenment contact us to reveal their unique spiritual truth.

Angels are the highest form of spiritual energy vibration, never having walked the earth in a physical form. They have always been spiritual beings working in the background to guide and protect us. When an angel intervenes, we often feel a powerful, hard-to-describe force behind the event. These moments may even be considered supernatural. Angels often channel through the living to assist or protect someone. They can inspire the minds of people to do good deeds.

I had my own angel experience several years ago. I was walking our dog with my partner and his mom through a neighborhood at sunset. As we turned a corner, we saw a young woman stumbling toward us from a park. Her white jeans were stained with blood, dirt, and grass. As we approached, we asked her if she was okay, and she could only mumble, "Help me." All of her front teeth were missing, and her mouth was bloodied. She collapsed in my mother-in-law's arms on the street curb. We called 911, waited for the ambulance, and watched this girl toggle between this world and the next. My mother-in-law held her in a warm embrace of love, telling her she would be okay. As she slipped in and out of consciousness, we continued to talk to her, trying to find out what happened while keeping her awake. I prayed at that moment for the young woman to survive. I felt this was her rock bottom, a turning point in her life. We later found out that she had been attacked by a group of people in the park and hit in the face with a beer bottle. I felt that whoever did this to her was nearby when we came upon her and only fled when they saw us. I know that angels were working in the background to ensure our paths crossed on that street. Spirit guided us to go on the walk that day. We did not have to walk through the neighborhood in that direction at that time. In fact, we usually went a different route, but we were pulled effortlessly in that direction together. There was also nobody else on the street, so no one else was there to help her.

This is how angels intervene with the living. They nudge the living to help those in the greatest need, often without our knowledge that it's happening. If we desire to serve others, angels will guide us in doing so. We may see an angel as a spark of light in its purest form of energy. Some people see them with wings and halos over their heads. But more often than not, they are working in the background unseen.

Be aware that just as angels are the highest vibration of energy nudging us to do good, there is also a darkness capable of manipulating the vulnerable to do horrible things when they are emotionally weighed down in a lower vibration of energy. These dark energies, often called "dark digits," are demons. Yes, demons exist, but whether they play a role in our lives depends on our choices and whether we give them attention. Demons are the lowest form of energy, and they connect with those on earth who welcome such energy or whenever someone becomes stuck in a cycle of poor choices and low self-worth. Demons enter our world through our pain and suffering. How well we keep up our spiritual hygiene determines whether they influence us. People who are morally bankrupt or allow their earthly ego to rule every aspect of their lives are easy targets for demons. Alcohol and harsh drugs tend to lower our vibration, making us more vulnerable and susceptible to these lower energies. Prayer, meditation, and positive self-talk guide us toward a higher vibration of protection. This is why meditation is part of my daily routine. I welcome the healing white light to surround me and those I love.

When I think about my spiritual web, I'm reminded of my support from birth. My mom had difficulty conceiving, and when she finally did, she struggled throughout her pregnancy with what the doctors referred to as a "risky pregnancy." However, she did not let this news interfere with her plan to be a mother. It was what she wanted most in life. I was born three months premature and weighed just two and a half pounds. I spent the first eight weeks in the ICU. Doctors and nurses referred to me as a "miracle baby" because my survival seemed unlikely. As difficult as my introduction was to this world, I am aware now that on a soul level my complicated birth was part of a much broader spiritual plan for my mom. Despite her addictions and the low vibration she put herself into with her substance abuse, her primary purpose was to bring me into this world, and her spirit guides and angels helped her. Family members have told me that my mom was never happier than during her pregnancy with me. She stopped using drugs and alcohol, which gave her a new perspective and hope for her life. When my mom died, everyone told me that one of the last things she said was that her most significant accomplishment was having me. This knowledge is a gift I carry with me always. It took an orchestra of souls and spiritual support to bring me here, for which I'm forever grateful.

After I was born, my struggles didn't end. I faced new

hurdles with parents who had profound challenges to overcome, but I know my spiritual web helped me navigate a difficult childhood, just as my dad's spiritual web eventually helped change him.

When my mom died, it was a wake-up call for my dad. I know she helped him from the other side to get out of that destructive lifestyle with drugs. She is a part of that spiritual web he and I share that guides and nudges us into new and better directions. And as crazy as it may sound to someone who doesn't see life from this spiritually connected level, my relationship with my mom is the best it's ever been. I'd even go as far as to say that our relationship truly began when she died. I may not physically see her anymore, but I can feel her presence every day. She shows me signs that she is with me and guiding me. I don't dwell on her earthly physical suffering anymore because I can see that it was all part of a larger blueprint, a spiritual agenda set forth by her and for her before she was ever born. Because I believe that and witness it continually through prayer, faith, and the undeniable evidence of the existence of an afterlife that comes through my channeling for others, I understand that we are never alone. I have faith that my spiritual web is always with me and lifting me during the most challenging times.

How we feel our spiritual web's presence may differ for each of us. Whether or not you feel this support network, it is there. If you remain open to it and learn to engage with it more fully, your life will profoundly transform. You will realize there are no limits to what you can accomplish because there is a whole realm that plays a role in your continued joy and happiness. Nothing in life is by mistake or coincidental; there is purpose to everything. There is a constant energy weaving in and out of our lives that divinely connects us to the people and situations we encounter. These are not chance encounters but opportunities to touch upon this deeper pervasive connection between us all. Those connections come from our spiritual web, which is continually working to help us thrive in this life and will surround us in our moment of transition into the next one.

DAILY PRACTICE

Calling Upon Your Spiritual Web for Guidance

This visualization practice engages with your spiritual team. The intention is to open yourself to signs that they are with you so you may feel their unlimited support throughout your daily life.

Meditation is a powerful tool, a sacred practice for calling upon our divine spiritual support network. It's also an opportunity to make deeper connections with our loved ones who've crossed over. All we need to do is ask, and they will be there to assist us. Our spiritual web is accessible through our heart center, where the realm of Spirit resides. Allow yourself to open your heart to the loving energy of your support network on the other side.

Start by getting into a comfortable position. Place your hands over your heart and leave them there throughout the meditation. Feel the support of your hands embracing your chest as you do this. Visualize a web of sparkling pink and white lights weaving in and out of your heart center. This is your light source connecting you to everything in the seen and unseen worlds. With each inhalation, see the web glow brighter and the connection stronger. Allow yourself to go deeper.

Visualize this light as it expands from your chest and fills the room. Notice how you feel uplifted by this glowing, supportive energy source. Your open-heart center is your doorway to your spiritual web, a place to greet those in the web from our world. Permit them to show you signs in this sacred moment, but let go of the need for a specific sign. Allow signs to come to you naturally, even unexpectedly. There's no timeframe or limits to how or when you will receive this sacred gift.

Feel the excitement of embarking on your journey to awareness. Know that your sign is on its way. This is your chance to gain trust in the power of your web. You'll know you've received a sign when you feel "a wink in the heart," like a soft "hello" from afar. When you recognize the sign, shift your awareness to your hands over your heart. Notice any physical sensations, like goosebumps or warmth. This physical manifestation validates your awareness, bringing the realm of Spirit into the physical world. You can have this active engagement with your guides, loved ones, angels, and ascended masters whenever you choose. Acknowledging these signs only strengthens your connection to this vast energy network.

As you build on this relationship with your spiritual web, more signs will reveal themselves over time in the most beautiful and unique ways. I highly encourage writing down your signs when you receive them so you can look upon them in times of need as a reminder that you are never alone.

Chapter 11

SETTING INTENTIONS

Every moment of your life is infinitely creative, and the universe
is endlessly bountiful. Just put forth a clear enough request,
and everything your heart truly desires must come to you.

— SHAKTI GAWAIN

One of the most underrated superpowers most of us don't even realize we have is the ability to manifest our desires into reality by setting intentions. An intention is a mental commitment to something that matters to us, a deliberate focus of our energy that presents opportunities to create a physical manifestation. We are such powerful beings of divine light that we have manifested ourselves into human form, projecting our intent from the other side like a lightning bolt into this world. Incredible, right? Imagine how transformative life could be if we use that same focused energy in our daily lives.

I state my intentions throughout my day, from the moment I awake. Sometimes I do it while I'm on the move, but most times, I try to find a quiet place and moment where I can pause and focus on what I want to bring to fruition. If I can, I light a candle. This helps set the mood and creates a symbolic manifestation of the intention in the physical world. Before I go into a reading, I state my intention to be of service as a clear vessel of validation and peace for my client. For a one-person private reading, it might take me a minute or less. For a larger group, like an audience reading, I may spend ten minutes visualizing the people present in the room with their hearts wide open, capable of receiving Spirit. I create a feeling of healing within myself and surrender to Spirit so that I may become a vessel for others.

At the start of each week, I write what I want to create that week, an energetic platform from which to launch. I might focus on trust, healing, or peace. When I enter that intention-setting space, I'm making mental deposits to create energy and an atmosphere that will set events into motion. Some might refer to an intention as a prayer. I see it as what is within my soul that I want to bring to the world, usually something that I have a significant passion for creating. While the two practices are similar, I see prayer as an active dialogue with our spiritual web, and intention-setting is the force behind that active dialogue that summons the energy to create the atmosphere of manifestation and attraction for what we seek. While our spiritual web certainly assists us in how our intention manifests, the intention is the origin of the desire itself. I may not know how it will happen, but that is the beautiful mystery of intention-setting. Setting the intention is the "what." The "how" will manifest as I continue to focus on what I want. By creating the atmosphere, the elements I need for my intention to manifest will eventually appear at the right time.

It's important to visualize the outcome of our intention.

By seeing our desire as if it has already happened, we create a mental space from which it will manifest. The excitement we feel from conjuring up our intention is the vibrational force necessary for it to manifest. It can be so powerful that whatever we choose to focus on can become our reality and attract more of the same. If we put forth the effort to set intentions for what we truly want, we can transform our lives.

In 2017, I did just that.

I've always enjoyed channeling for people, but in 2017 I felt the need to do something more with my gift. I had been teaching a one-day workshop on developing psychic and intuitive gifts for several years. I loved the experience of showing people how my gift worked and how we all have access to the other side in unique ways. I was moved to see other people experience their own aha moment when they made that personal connection with Spirit. I knew how transformative the workshop could be for people, so I wanted to expand upon it and offer a multiple-day workshop experience.

I set my intention to find a way to share my knowledge and experiences of connecting with Spirit in other ways. I spent each day in my meditation room, visualizing myself teaching a room of people about this subject matter. I envisioned the scene surrounded by a glow of white light, which helped set my pure intention into motion. After a few months of practicing my daily intention-setting, I received an email from one of the country's top spiritual wellness retreat centers. They wanted me to teach my workshop as a weekend course at their center. This led to other retreat centers contacting me, and before I knew it, I was asked to teach at multiple centers nationwide. The truly transformative part of what happened throughout these workshops was the healing and connection people made with each other and me. It allowed me to step into my own with my gift by sharing it in a whole new way.

For an intention to manifest, it must be free of ego and serve the highest good of all involved. Setting an intention for harm to be brought to someone you don't like only attracts the harm back to you. Setting an intention for someone who doesn't love you to fall in love with you will not work, as this is not in alignment with their intentions or their highest good. Spirit does not work that way. The intention must be pure. Some of the most rewarding parts of intentions are how they can affect the lives of those around us in meaningful ways.

At the start of 2019, I had set an intention to have a travel experience that was deeply meaningful and would allow me to feel more connected spiritually. I left the how and when open. So, when my partner, Patrick, asked me in December if I wanted to go to the island of Kaua'i with his parents, I jumped at the opportunity. I had been to the Big Island before, but never to Kaua'i. This was my sign.

In the years leading up to this, I had developed the practice of reciting Hindu chants. So, before the trip, I continually meditated and chanted, setting the intention for us all to have a meaningful, spiritually connected experience on the trip together. I asked that this be of the highest good for all, something unique and uplifting we would never forget.

We didn't plan activities for this trip in advance, embracing the idea of letting go and letting the experience take us where we were meant to be. While there, I was taken in by the unique beauty of this island, abundant with waterfalls and blanketed in greenery from the mountains to the beaches. It's a sleepier island, mostly locals, with a quieter nightlife and far fewer tourists than the other islands of Hawai'i. So, I knew going into this it would be a different kind of vacation. And with less opportunity to lie on the beach soaking up the hot sun, I'd hoped to find a deeper, more meaningful experience from the island.

During our stay in the quaint town of Kapaʻa, Patrick and I went on a morning walk along the beach boardwalk and stumbled upon a local diner, a unique place that served things like lavender-infused iced coffee. While Kapaʻa is one of the more populated areas of Kauaʻi, it still has a small-town feel and is not your typical Hawaiian tourist trap, which I loved. You can meet locals and see a side of Hawaiʻi you don't always get on the Big Island. And there are roosters everywhere! Like urban pigeons, they dominate their landscape. While at breakfast that morning, our waitress — who was very open and full of positive energy — asked if we'd been to Kauaʻi's Hindu Monastery. "I didn't even know you had a monastery," I replied. She said, "It's the best-kept secret on the island. It was a life-changing experience for me. You need to go." When we checked into it, we were able to reserve a time. It books up quickly, so we were fortunate to get a spot. We'd been struggling to schedule activities, so this felt like a sign that we were supposed to go.

We drove to the top of a mountain, which had breathtaking ocean views, and entered this beautiful natural setting, which included statues of Hindu gods, ornate gardens, and a rudraksha forest, which are towering trees with enormous roots. It was like stepping into an ancient world, like nothing I'd ever seen. After exploring the monastery grounds, we came upon the monastery itself, surrounded by fountains and elaborate gardens. This mountaintop sanctuary has some of the best views of waterfalls the island has to offer.

Inside the monastery, a Hindu ceremony was underway in

the Kadavul Temple. Exploring the grounds, we were drawn toward the sounds of chanting inside the temple. A crowd of visitors was outside removing their shoes and crossing the threshold. Inspired to do the same, we followed them, open for whatever awaited us. I was utterly taken aback by the ornate beauty inside with bursts of color in the decor, the delightful aroma of frankincense in the air, the glimmering statues of Hindu gods lining the walls, and the overall uplifting energy of the cultural rituals being performed. People laid offerings of flowers at the front of the room near what looked to be an altar. At different points, they kneeled, prayed, and chanted along with the monk seated near the offerings. The joy one felt in the room was infectious. Everywhere we turned, people looked happy just to be there.

Everyone in our group, including Patrick's parents, participated in the part of the ceremony that involved writing down our intentions and the things we wanted to release from our lives. We didn't know any of this would be happening when we arrived, but we quickly joined in these rituals because it felt so right. No judgment. No fear. Just pure presence in this magical experience, which no one expected but which couldn't have been more spot-on with what I'd hoped we would find. I was already living my intentions with these practices, which is why it showed up for me as validation that I was on the right path for my spiritual wellness. It also gave my in-laws a firsthand look at what I practice every day, and it helped them appreciate the power of intention. Before we arrived in Kaua'i, I didn't know how my intention would come to fruition or how quickly, but I trusted that it would, and it did.

What's the takeaway with intention-setting? That it is not a genie in a bottle. It's not the old "I'll grant you three wishes" adage from storybooks. It takes dedication, faith, and an open-ness to a connection with a higher power. On a fundamental level, just merely giving your focus to something reinforces it, pulling it further into your orbit (as I discuss earlier). But by repeatedly focusing on what you want to accomplish, you cre-ate a deliberate energetic attraction for that personal change. This is the magic of intention-setting. With this practice, you set into motion the attractive force between you and your desire. Things unfold that align with your intention, inspiring you to put your desire into action. The signposts along the way become undeniable. That's where the magic lies behind all this. You feel it on an intuitive level, and when you have all that working together, anything is possible.

DAILY PRACTICE

The Crystal Ball of Intention

This visualization exercise practices intention-setting by calling upon the white light to assist in charging the intention for man-ifestation.

Find a safe and comfortable space with privacy and no dis-tractions. Sit upright with your palms faceup. This places you in both a receiving and a sending position. As you inhale, close your eyes and focus on your breath. As you exhale, say to yourself out loud the word *relax*. Repeat this process and take your time; keep going until you reach a relaxed state. You're stripping away the outside world as you focus on the stillness within.

Visualize a crystal ball in front of you, a bubble of white light. Focus on the entire ball. Hold it in your hands. You may feel a buzzing energy from it. This is the creation energy of the Universe, from where possibility is born. It is a window into your future, your desires, and all that is you. This is your magical intention oracle. If you need to refocus at any time, repeat the breathing exercise above. Allow the light from the crystal ball to envelop you. As you blend with this pure white light, focus inward on this bright space where anything is possible.

Now, visualize your intention playing out in this magic window in your life. Play it repeatedly, studying the formation of this intention down to the details — who's involved, what's involved, the actions taking place for it, the setting where it plays out. Become immersed in this intention. Notice how this scene makes you feel as it brings positive feelings of success, happiness, and peace. Allow your feelings to fuel your desire and visualization. As you inhale, the white light becomes brighter and brighter until all you see is the light. Visualize the light flowing out of the top of your head as it connects to the larger Universe. This light is your energy charger, like plugging into the main grid. Charge your intention with this pure energy source while surrendering all that no longer serves you to the light for transformation. When you're ready, snap your fingers three times to return to the room and open your eyes. Thank the Universe for delivering what you seek through its limitless bounty of energy.

Know that after each repetition of this exercise, intention-setting will become second nature to you. It will only take a moment to visualize your intention and send it into the Universe for creation.

Chapter 12

THE MYSTICAL POWER
IN MANTRAS

*Mantras are passwords that transform
the mundane into the sacred.*

— DEVA PREMAL

Mystical words, phrases, or utterances with distant and often unknown origins from deep in the past fascinate humanity today. Perhaps as our culture has evolved over the centuries and embraced science and provable facts over sensing and intuition, we've lost a universal and fundamental part of being human — our connection to the invisible world, to Spirit. Just because something is not currently provable by science doesn't mean it has no value or won't be proven later. A revival is underway right now — a broader yearning — to access this connection to our innate spirituality. Adopting mantras is part of that, but what does that mean?

A mantra is a word, phrase, or sound repeated continually to help concentrate or set an intention. Mantras can lift our vibration and turn our mental space around rapidly. We can chant mantras anywhere, whether in a quiet setting, like in the privacy of our home, speaking them aloud; or in a crowded setting, like waiting in line at the store, reciting them in our mind. Their power resides in our intention, and thoughts hold just as much power as spoken words. The concept of uttering these simple words or phrases to reach enlightened states of consciousness dates back thousands of years. The word *mantra* comes from ancient Sanskrit in India. Its meaning has many interpretations, which is another reason why it is so mystical. It most likely came from combining two words: *manas*, meaning "the mind," and *tra*, most likely meaning "a tool." Various religions and cultures have adopted mantras over time. They are our bridge to the invisible world, connecting us deeper with the pervasive energy of the Universe, where manifestation arises.

I've always been fascinated by the mystical origin of mantras. However, it wasn't until I made mantras a regular part of my daily meditations that I started to see the impact these repeated sounds have on my overall well-being. I notice a tingling, elevating, peaceful feeling when I repeat these words or phrases. I repeat them in my mind and out loud throughout the day. The process is similar to giving gratitude, where repetition keeps us focused on positive thoughts and connects us more deeply with the realm of Spirit. Repeating a mantra stills my mind while pulling me into my heart's center and into a greater awareness of the buzzing energy around me. In this energetic space, I am highly focused, my consciousness expands, and my chakras activate.

I've used mantras for many years. Often I use simple phrases for what I want to experience within my reality, such as "I am love," "I am healthy," or "I am limitless." I see mantras much like an outfit. I start each day by looking in the closet and pulling out what I want to wear that will make me feel my best. I ask myself, "Which word or phrase do I want to repeat that will lift my vibration so I can experience more positivity by calling in this energy for my day?" Like "flipping the negatives," I am reprogramming my mind to align with my higher self by using simple, positive phrases for attraction.

While I still use mantras, I've been drawn toward daily chanting in recent years because of how high it raises my vibration. This led me to *chant* mantras, specifically Vedic chants, and I searched for as many of them as possible. Chanting mantras is often done in Buddhism and Hinduism for ascension into heightened states of consciousness and an overall sense of well-being. These ancient mantras took my meditations to a new level, deeper into the fundamental vibration of sound.

Most people are familiar with the word *om*, which is a mantra. *Om* is often used in yoga. It is uttered at the beginning or end to achieve a peaceful balance of the mind and body. It is believed to be the vibrational sound of the Universe, the all-encompassing background sound of everything. You can use it on its own or at the beginning of other mantras, as there are many more to choose from. *Om* gives me an acute sense of awareness, and the vibration reverberates throughout my third eye — clairvoyance — keeping it clear of any energetic debris.

By 2015, I had been practicing meditation for many years, but I yearned for something that would take me deeper into it, which is when I discovered chanting. My path to this practice was paved by signs that led me to it. During meditation one day, I saw an elephant. From there, I soon saw elephants everywhere throughout my day. Intrigued by what this could mean, I investigated the symbolism of elephants, which led me to the Hindu deity Ganesh. Ganesh has the head of an elephant, four arms, and is known for removing obstacles and bringing wisdom, good luck, and new beginnings. I had heard of Ganesh but didn't fully know who he was and what he stood for. Understanding the power of Ganesh for transformation drew me deeper into chanting these mystical mantras.

As I learned more about Ganesh, I discovered the chant "Om Gam Ganapataye Namaha," which is for removing obstacles and bringing peace, clarity, and abundance. The discovery of this chant inspired me to extend my meditative practice to include chanting. The power I felt from this mantra was transformative. It created within me a new and more positive state of mind. My days unfolded more frequently with ease, and I noticed roadblocks dissolved. Eventually, I increased this practice until I was reciting 108 chants per day, the number of beads on a mala. From a practical standpoint, the beads are used to keep track of how many mantras we've recited. I see their purpose as a way to bring the spiritual into physical form. Once I began this new way of meditating, it felt like all stagnant energy debris around me was swept away. With this new state of mind, I was cleansed of worries and had created an atmosphere of positive energy around me.

Today, I don't limit my chants to 108 if I feel the need to do more — and that's especially true when I travel. I have always been a nervous flier, so as soon as I board the plane, I close my eyes and chant in my mind. Even recited in my head, the mantras take on a harmonious sound that brings a sense of calm and peace, where I feel a deeper support from my spiritual web. I pulled out my mala beads once while traveling on one of my regular trips to New York, and the lady next to me noticed.

"Oh, wow!" she exclaimed. "You use mala beads?"

Not too many people I run into know what they are. When I told her that I use them to chant to Ganesh, she was shocked. She said she does the same thing every time she flies, since she is a nervous flier, too. What were the odds that we would be seated next to each other? Before that flight took off, we chanted to Ganesh out loud, and the additional support made me feel even safer. It was nice to have my practice validated by someone who understood how comforting such a ritual could be.

With what I do every day — channeling Spirit for others — I am undoubtedly affected by the heavy hearts of those I work with. I would not trade that for anything in the world, but I must be careful to clear out those heavier energies and find balance by releasing that energy while restoring my own. That's why I also chant in the evenings if I feel tired or drained, to remove old energy and bring in the new. Given my music background, adding this sound element to my daily meditation feels natural, since it's an extension of something I am already familiar with — how to reach higher vibrations through sound. But you don't need to have a music background to appreciate reciting mantras. Chanting mantras can be used by anyone to tap into the unlimited energy source of the Universe through the vibration of sound for a more positive state of well-being.

Mantras give us in-depth focus. They help direct our energy into the presence of Spirit by disconnecting us from our ego. Mantras bring about a feeling of uninhibited flow from within, something truly magical. They help us see life as it was intended, that we are an eternal soul manifested into human form. Many use mantras to elevate their souls and connect with higher energy vibrations. Some use them to manifest something tangible, like wealth. It's all about using that vibration to attract desired elements toward us. Mantras can bring radical change on many levels. Because they pull us into the present moment, they can help us recognize the beauty all around: a gorgeous sunset, a beautiful flower, or a graceful bird soaring above. These moments of appreciation are priceless in all their forms and can heighten our awareness of the connection between us and everything around us.

DAILY PRACTICE

Introductory Guide to the Mystical Mantras

Below is my list of go-to chants. Through the mysticism of these ancient mantras, you raise your vibration after each reciting to bring about positive attraction, overall well-being, transformation, and peace.

When reciting any mantra, it's important to set the intention for transformation. Like turning the key in the ignition before driving, it ignites the spark necessary to bring about change. When possible, I like to create a sacred atmosphere for reciting a mantra, like lighting a candle or incense and dimming the lights in the room. But mantras and chanting can be recited anywhere.

I highly recommend investing in a mala and using the 108 beads to keep track of the mantras. However, it's possible to use rosaries or other strings of beads, but these might make it more challenging to keep track of all 108 repetitions of the mantra.

With your mala or beads, sit comfortably with your feet rooted to the floor. Keep your spine straight, as if you were an antenna for energy to flow from the top down. I recommend closing your eyes to leave the physical sense of self behind while chanting your mantra.

- **Om:** This is the pervasive sound of the Universe that brings about peace, positivity, stillness, and focus. This is a great starting place to sense the hum of the Universe flowing within and outside you. Within seconds, this simple mantra can clear your mind, detach you from the worries of the external world, open your awareness to your higher self, and activate your third eye (clairvoyance).
- **Om Namaha Shivaya** [pronounced: om-na-ma-ha-shi-vai-ya]: The Shiva mantra, a bow to the all-knowing self, clears karmic energy from the past, connects you with your divine self, brings about confidence, and strengthens from within.
- **Om Gam Ganapataye Namaha** [pronounced: om-gam-gan-a-pat-ah-yay-na-ma-ha]: The Ganesh mantra removes obstacles from within and outside of yourself and attracts success, good health, and happiness. This is an excellent mantra to use when you're looking for a successful outcome to something, like starting a new business, before an important meeting, or embarking on a new move.
- **Om Shanti Om** [pronounced: om-shahn-tee-om]: The peace mantra brings a sense of peace to mind, body, and spirit, affecting all areas of one's life — including the past. This is not limited to yourself; you can use it to bring peace to others. This is a great mantra to use before going into meditation or prayer.

- **Soham** [pronounced: so-hum]: The "I am that" mantra balances mind and body, inspires happiness, and redirects you to your eternal self and existence in many realms at once while creating presence through physical harmony. It is often used in yoga and repeated internally as a reflection of our breathing process (*so* for the inhale and *hum* for the exhale). Repeating it out loud, you may feel a powerful resonance in your crown or third-eye chakra.

I encourage you to research other mantras that inspire you. These are a few of my favorites. Let your intuition be your guide for expanding upon these.

Chapter 13

INTUITION AND
A LESSON IN TRUST

*The more you trust your intuition, the more empowered you become,
the stronger you become, and the happier you become.*

— GISELE BÜNDCHEN

That gut feeling, that uneasiness in the pit of your stomach,
that choice to suddenly take a different route home —
these are not random or arbitrary thoughts and shouldn't be
ignored. They are examples of our intuition, or higher self, trying to reach us. I've discussed what intuition is, but how do we
tune in to it? And how do we know we can trust it?

To tap into our intuition, we must first learn to rise above
thought to access the other side. Like the electrical current
of a radio signal traveling from a transmitter to an antenna,
we must tune in to the channel on our own radio to receive
information. Tuning in to that signal is the key to living our
best life. It can be easier said than done, but the principle is

simple. Our intuition should be as natural as our breath, but the programming from the outside world has scrambled the signal. Sometimes we need to turn the dial a few times to find the right station. Once we do, we know exactly what to do the next time we want to access that information.

To heighten our intuition, we need to get out of our own way — out of our rampant thoughts — and listen to the broadcast coming from within. This is our personal channel, one strengthened by a deeper trust in oneself. By decluttering our minds and learning how to be still in moments when we need guidance, we can reinforce that trust in our intuition. We have all heard stories about people making decisions that seem, in the moment, to be random or even absurd. But because they trusted their intuition, everything worked out. This is not a coincidence. It is divine intervention guiding us.

Everything you have read to this point — connecting with your inner child, letting go, giving gratitude, the daily practices — is grounded in intuition and connected to your energy source. The exercises at the end of each chapter are purposeful and designed to help you access information from within. The visualization techniques are a way to dial in to your innate clairvoyance. Utilizing intuition every day is like building a muscle or the third eye. It becomes stronger as our fear-based doubts diminish. Some might call it our inner voice, our higher self, the voice of God, or the voice of Spirit. Whatever you call it, it is your connection to the divinity within you.

We all entered this world with the gift of intuition. It's part of our fabric, whether we acknowledge it or not. The problem is that people often ignore this part of themselves. Because we live in a world obsessed with proof, many people lose touch with their intuition or learn not to trust it. But it's always accessible, even if we think it's gone. It never leaves us.

Following our intuition, even when it seems absurd, can lead to beautiful and transformative changes in our lives. I know this to be true from an experience in 2015. Patrick and I bought our first home together in Southern California, but after living there for barely more than a year, my gut instinct told me it was time for us to move. We lived in a home we loved, but we wanted something bigger. I contacted our realtor, Chris, and told him we were ready to sell the house. He knew I was a psychic medium, so he wasn't shocked when I told him I had a vision of who would buy it.

"It's going to be a single woman whose dad will be helping her with the purchase," I said. "She's young, has red hair, and loves to cook."

About a week after listing our house, Chris called to say he had a woman interested in seeing it, and he would show it to her that evening. After the showing, he called to tell us he was pretty sure it was the woman I described to him. He said she was young with red hair, loved to cook, and our newly remodeled kitchen would be ideal for her. Her father was also with her because he was helping her with the purchase.

Intuition is spontaneous energy. It can feel exciting in the moment because we're shifting our awareness into something magical and otherworldly conjured up from that divine realm. Seeing this woman enter our home was confirmation that we were doing the right thing by moving. It was no shock that she ultimately bought our home.

This left us with one problem, though: Patrick and I hadn't bought a new house yet. Aside from wanting more space, we hoped to find a home similar to what we had. So, when our realtor took us to one that was precisely that — down to the paint colors and vaulted ceilings — my intuition kicked into overdrive. I knew we had found the one, and Patrick agreed.

"But Bill," Chris said to me, "there are ten other people putting bids in for it." He told us that we had to submit our best and final offer.

"Give us a couple of hours," I told him. I needed to meditate on this big decision. I knew it had to be the right offer or we would lose the house. In meditation, I asked Spirit point-blank to tell me what we needed to do to get this home. Within seconds of going within and asking Spirit for guidance, I saw a specific number in my mind's eye — sixty thousand dollars over the asking price! I was astonished, but I could not shake that number from my mind. When I discussed it with Patrick, we agreed to do it. As crazy as the amount seemed, I had to follow my intuition.

Chris called me that evening while I was at my office and said he needed to know our offer. When I told him, he was stunned. He said although we needed to be above the asking price, since the house was priced below market value, he thought we were way too high. He politely tried to talk us down, but I insisted on that amount. I felt that I needed to trust the information I had received, despite what anyone else thought. So, he submitted our bid that night with the offer I requested.

He called us back the next day.

"Bill, I'm glad we went with your gut. A couple of bids came very close to your offer, but you were the only one at your price. If you'd offered even one dollar less, you would've lost the house. Congratulations! It's yours!"

This was a significant moment in trust for me. Most people would've considered us crazy for that offer, but it was the right amount. None of what happened was coincidental or luck. From the start of this process, I trusted the guidance I was receiving from the other side — from when I told Patrick it was time for us to move to putting in the offer on the house we loved. The more I trusted that inner guidance, the more the information came to me with each step. But what is also important to note is not every answer I was seeking came instantly. They took time. My first spark of intuition came when I felt guided that we sell our house, and it took months to complete the sale and then purchase a new one. Then I felt a girl with red hair would buy it, and then I felt the specific amount for the bid. The more I trusted, the more I received.

Our intuition is not cut and dry; it's more of an art form, like a painter who sits down in front of a blank canvas. The painter doesn't necessarily know at the start what they are going to paint, but they trust their intuitive guidance to create, their skills as a painter, and their ability to be inspired spontaneously. That's how our intuition and clairvoyance work. When we trust in ourselves, we trust our ability to shape and enhance our lives. And that's all we have to do — be true to the voice within. It's simpler than we think. We must not let overthinking block us. If we can remove the layers of our humanness — our impatience, doubt, need for approval, and earthly ego — we can access a higher frequency where our greater potential lies. This is how we can cocreate with the Universe the life we want.

The challenge in learning to trust ourselves is that it's a fine line we walk between our intuition and ego. Which one are we listening to? It's a constant dance between our higher self and our ego self. Like walking along a tightrope, we are continually rebalancing between those two parts of us. Are we making that impulse purchase because we feel our intuition is telling us to or because our ego is saying so? Are we dating this guy because our intuition tells us he's "the one" or because our ego is blinded by his good looks? The only way to tell the difference is by practicing trust in oneself, much like the tightrope walker must trust in their ability to focus on the task at hand. Think of it this way: Intuition comes in the fraction of a second before thought. By the time thoughts arise, it's too late. That's ego. Listen for the space in between the initial emotional reaction and the thought. This requires some trial and error, but you'll eventually be able to discern between that inner voice and your ego self.

Your higher self can't reach you if your ego is trying to control everything. That's why it's important to meditate and connect with your higher power. I do this before I give any reading. I visualize that white light, that sacred space, to ensure I'm connected to the other side and communicating messages to clients from their loved ones. I call it the Christ light. It's a pure, protective, omnipresent energy source that opens my intuitive antenna for receiving. It helps me forget all my ego thoughts, step out of my own way, and trust what I am about to receive.

I discuss how to trust intuition in my workshops, and I love how personal the experience of intuitive work can be. People enter these workshops with different skill sets, intentions, and backgrounds, but they all share a desire to learn how to trust more deeply in themselves. This is why intuitive work is so transformative — it allows us to face who we really are, get vulnerable, and trust our connection to the other side. That's the magic — building personal strength and connection.

Many people don't think they can connect with their higher self and the other side. They don't think they have the ability to do it. But they do. They amaze themselves by the end of the workshop because they finally see we are all connected to an infinite realm that guides us to live our best life. That trust in oneself that I teach about is a process. It's not over after people walk away from the course; they must continue to practice and do the work. And we can't get discouraged if we think we've gotten something wrong.

Intuiting information is not a perfect science. I refer to the information I receive when channeling as being like broken shards of glass that must be reassembled to reveal the whole picture or message. Spirit only gives us glimpses of information from the other side, and sometimes it may not always be clear in the moment. The value we place on time and timelines is a human perspective, as there is no linear time on the other side. Everything we feel, even if we don't know what it means in the moment, will connect with everything else and eventually reveal its significance. But this requires trust that we are being led to where we are supposed to go. The download we receive as a channel is as unique as the person interpreting the shards of that information. When we intuit, often it is our own lives that act as a reference point when interpreting the message. The trust we place in ourselves and in Spirit is the key to unlocking the magic of intuition.

DAILY PRACTICE

A Sense-Shifting Impression for Deeper Guidance

This visualization and writing practice builds trust in your intuition and helps you differentiate ego thought from intuitive sensing.

In this practice, we focus on two different senses, the human sense of hearing and the intuitive sight (known as clairvoyance). By shifting our focus from one sense to another, we distract our rational ego mind long enough to recognize intuitive information surfacing from within before we have time to judge and analyze it. This is the intuitive download. For this exercise, you need something that emits sound, preferably a white noise, like tranquil music or a fan.

To start, ask yourself what you most need guidance for in your life — such as a change of career, a move, having another child, and so on. Write this down. Keep this in the back of your mind while you begin your visualization.

Close your eyes with your palms facing up in receiving mode. Call upon your spiritual web to support, protect, and guide you during the exercise. Practice the deep breathing techniques you've learned in previous exercises to get into a relaxed and calm space. Once you are relaxed, visualize a screen of white light before you, like a large white projector screen. This is your backdrop for your intuitive download.

Shift your focus to the white noise sound. Give yourself time to practice your deep breathing with the sound as your focus. Then shift your attention from the sound back to the large white projector screen in your mind. If you don't have anything on the screen the first time, continue to shift between the sound and the screen until you notice imagery, trusting and documenting even the simplest of visions.

What do you see, feel, or sense? The flash of information you receive in the fraction of a second in between thoughts is your download. Don't forget to trust your first impressions! Once you feel you've received enough information, write notes for anything you visualized. There is no wrong answer here. No matter how absurd it seems, document what you experience.

After your visualization practice, interpret what you have sensed. This is the time to use rational thought. If you feel stuck, continue practicing your breathing technique and repeat the process of switching back and forth between these separate sensory inputs.

Keep these notes and see in time how events unfold.

For some people, this practice may feel more advanced. Don't get discouraged. If you need more practice, revisit some of the earlier exercises before coming back to this one.

Chapter 14

CUTTING CORDS

Fools take a knife and stab people in the back. The wise take a knife,
cut the cord, and free themselves from the fools.

— ANONYMOUS

A t this very moment, you are being pulled by an energetic
force toward something you may not be aware of, much
the way gravity pulls all things together. When we connect
emotionally with anything, part of our energy attaches to that
person or situation, present or past; it's all the same. This is
called an energy cord, a concept in metaphysics that asserts we
have invisible strands of energy tethering us to other people
and situations. Simply put, human connection is an emotional
connection that ties us to each other, regardless of the time or
space in between. We are attached to other people nonstop
all day — in our homes, on the road, at work, in stores, on the
phone, through social media, while taking a walk. We're *al-*
ways connected. And with those connections comes an energy

exchange. The question with each connection is: *Is it good energy or bad energy?* The choice is ours to attach or detach. If we cling to something negative and don't try to disconnect, that energy will stay with us endlessly and potentially affect other connections we make.

As a channel for Spirit, I purposely connect with the energy of others, so I must take extra care to protect my energy before and after a reading. When I first started out, I wasn't aware that the heaviness of emotions I felt afterward wasn't mine but rather those of the people for whom I read. The energy between them and their loved ones on the other side was so strong that it attached to me — the conduit for their energy exchange — and followed me into my personal life. Once I realized what was happening, I knew I needed to practice a brief visualization after each reading to cut those energy cords, which I felt attached to me through my solar plexus. When visualizing these cords, I often see them in different shapes, sizes, and colors, depending on the attachment. Some may be thin like hair, others thicker like a solid braided rope. Some may look golden or white, like light beams, while others may look black or brown, like dead roots.

Energy cords can affect even the most mundane daily tasks. Think about how easy it is to get attached to someone else's energy when you're frustrated with a situation.

For example, say you need to call a customer-service department because you have a problem with a recent purchase. Many companies outsource their call centers overseas, and English might not be the first language of the person you talk to. If this causes you to struggle to be understood, this can exacerbate an already frustrating situation. As your frustration grows, both of you may lose patience or become aggravated,

and the energy between you will become muddied and en-
twined. Though you are thousands of miles away, your energy
cords are connected. Even after hanging up the phone, the
energy cords remain attached.

This is why we must make cutting negative cords part of
our daily spiritual hygiene, no different from cleansing our
bodies by bathing each day. Unless we consciously remove
them, these strands of stagnant energy remain attached to us.
These cords arise even without a direct interaction. Someone
could cut us off on the highway and anger us — and a cord
attaches to us. Someone could write an editorial in the paper
that sparks our emotions — there's another cord. A person
could post something on social media that gets under our
skin — yet another cord.

Some people may experience an unhealthy friendship that
binds them to toxic energy cords. They may find themselves
depleted or emotionally hurt after interacting with this person,
yet be unaware of the dysfunction of the relationship. Awareness is the first step to healing from this. Most times, these
relationships tend to tip on the side of one person controlling
the friendship. This lack of balance creates tight, inflexible energy cords that keep us bound to the person through feelings
of low self-worth or manipulation.

The best way to test the strength of any relationship is to
go within, visualize the two of you standing together, and see
what those cords look like. Are they heavy, thick, knotted, and
dark? Or are they light, thin, and movable? If the cords feel
negative, it may be time to cut them. You don't need to cut the
person out of your life, if that's not what you want. The point is
not to get rid of the person; it's to sever what no longer serves
you in the relationship. If the person you've cut the energy

cord with eventually leaves or ends the relationship, that's their choice — just as it's your choice to create an emotional boundary between you. This protects you from this person's negative energy. There are some relationships where it's impossible to completely cut a person out of your life, like with a coworker or an in-law. In cases like this, cutting energy cords between you is how to create the emotional boundary you need while maintaining your power within the relationship.

Jan, a friend of mine, was a successful manager in the healthcare industry. One day, she told me how frustrated she was at work because of a toxic coworker, a nurse in her department. It was a delicate matter because Jan, though in a position of power, was not this woman's direct manager. Jan felt the nurse was undermining her authority, belittling her in subtle ways about her leadership, and creating excess work for her. She brought it up with the nurse's manager, but nothing improved, and Jan felt stuck. She did not want to risk escalating the situation by involving higher-ups and creating more problems.

I told Jan she must sever those toxic energy cords that bound her to this woman. I told her to visualize the nurse as happy, joyful, and surrounded by a glow of white light and to send this woman love. This is difficult to do when we are upset with someone, but it really does work to break cords. I suggested she see herself swiftly cutting the energy cords between them while saying a loving goodbye and to practice this every time she saw or thought of her. Jan found it hard to imagine that anything would resolve this broken relationship, but she practiced this visualization technique regularly over the next month. Later, she told me that she felt much more positive at work and at home after about a week or two of practicing it. She no longer felt emotionally tethered to this woman and could maintain a professional relationship without having negative feelings toward her.

Cutting cords is not a way of avoiding pain or difficult emotions. It's not an easy way out of challenging relationships, ones that might be worthwhile if the challenges can be overcome. It's a self-check to know where your energy is going and what is coming in.

When I need to reflect inward on my emotional energy cords, I call upon the archangel Michael, who is often depicted carrying a sword. If I see any black cords, I focus on them and ask Michael to slash those cords with his sword to return my energy to me. I call this "active visualization," which is part of our intuitive source that lets us disconnect those energies. Once the cord is cut, I usually feel the shift instantly and can breathe easier. This has served me well throughout my life, especially related to the traumatic events of my childhood. As I mention, energy cords relate not just to the present but to energies in the past as well. Sometimes, even after I cut a cord once, it can still feel attached, so I cut it again. Cords can be habitually ingrained in us and continue to reattach. Just thinking about something bad that happened can re-create that connection. This is why cord-cutting must be a continuous practice. By building an awareness of what negative energy does to us, our intuition grows stronger as we become more deeply connected to our energy source — our higher self. By reflecting within, removing unwanted energies, and taking charge of our feelings, we can thrive in any relationship because we no longer allow others to deplete our energy source. Our energy source is unbreakable.

Energy cords also relate to events. They attach from

anything we see or read about in the news, and without energetic boundaries, negativity and drama can become addictive. If we spend hours a day watching cable news or checking our newsfeed, we often don't realize that we have allowed this into our energy sphere, as we have normalized this behavior within ourselves.

War is a common example, such as the 2022 Russian invasion of Ukraine. Yes, it's important to be informed and to know what's happening in the world, but it's easy to tune in to war each day as if it were a television drama. We watch in terror as the most horrific atrocities unfold, but that doesn't fix anything or help the people suffering. If we recognize that we are watching the news solely in order to satisfy our need for drama, we are doing a disservice to ourselves. This is why it's important to cut our energy cords from certain world events. It doesn't mean we stick our heads in the sand and pretend nothing is happening, that everything is normal, but we set up boundaries that limit how much of that energy we let in. Imagine it like a valve on a faucet. Decide how much to let flow toward you and when to turn it off. When we turn the drama into positive action, such as giving donations or volunteering, we can turn the energy cords attached to us into something meaningful while freeing ourselves from their harmful effects. This is a way to transform energy cords.

The energy cords attached to us remain even after someone physically dies. They can even grow stronger, which can be positive or negative, depending on the situation. This came up for me when I had a cord-cutting session with my friend Shannon, an intuitive healer. We discovered that I had cords attached to the version of my mom I knew as a child. Obviously,

I have a deep love connecting me to the earthly version of my mom, but traumas were also associated with this attachment. Those negative attachments were periodically draining my power source. Shannon discerned a list of attachments I had with my mom and situations from our past that were creating emotional roadblocks. These roadblocks were caused by energy cords I was holding unknowingly. By recognizing them, she severed my attachment to the negativity associated with that part of my past. Afterward, I felt a renewed sense of well-being.

Whether on your own or with someone else's assistance, consistent cord-cutting can be a powerful practice for restoring your inner energy source and harmonizing your relationships.

I believe we are energy first before we are a physical body, and when we nourish our energy self (our higher self), we can change how we relate to others and situations. Knowing how to protect, deflect, and create energy boundaries through cord-cutting and projecting love is vital to our spiritual health.

Energy cords are not always bad, either. Our energy cords connect us to the ones we love most in this life and on the other side. They tend to be strong yet flexible cords, which lift and inspire us when we reflect upon them. This is how we know they are pure. These valuable energy connections have no geographical limitations. If you have a relationship you want to nurture more deeply, you can practice sending loving energy to that person whenever you like by visualizing your cords vibrating with a beam of pink light between the two of you. Once you start recognizing these powerful energy cords, you will learn how vital it is to keep your spiritual hygiene clean and your connections strong.

Cutting Cords to Protect Your Energy Boundaries

This grounding meditation visualization can assist in severing negative energy cords with others, so you establish an energetic boundary.

Cord-cutting is a type of energy work, and it's important to ground ourselves before starting any visualization practice. Grounding is essential in any energy work because it allows us to recognize that although we are engaging with other people's energy fields, we should always remain in control of our energy source.

You may already know with whom or what you want to cut cords. If not, call upon your spiritual web to assist you with any intuitive downloads you may need for this process and to visualize the cords in the best way possible.

It works best to focus on one person or event at a time during this exercise. If multiple people or situations come up, focus on the first one that comes to mind. You can spend time with each of them individually later. This may take more time than one session, so when you're done, write down anything you receive during the practice so you can return to it. During this process, you may feel a heaviness in your chest or belly. That's okay. It is more validation that the cords are attached.

Start by sitting upright in a comfortable position with your palms facing up on your lap. Close your eyes to go within. As in previous exercises, focus on deep breathing. I always recommend at least three deep breaths to reach a calm and relaxed state of being.

Visualize a glow of white light around your body. This energy field is your etheric body, where all energy connections take place. In your mind's eye, look down at your hands, your palms still facing up. You are in receiving mode, connected to your energy source. See and feel what this energy field emanating from you looks like. It might vibrate, buzz, or feel warm. Whatever you sense is okay. There is no right or wrong way to sense your own energy.

Now, visualize a glow of golden light around your solar plexus, the area below your diaphragm and above your navel. Like lightning that strikes a rod, this golden light travels down and out the base of your spine, through your root chakra, and into Mother Earth. This is your grounding cord. See it like a thick root traveling effortlessly into the depths of the earth. As it reaches deeper, it travels miles into the center of our planet. Feel stable and supported by the nurturing embrace of Mother Earth. Allow any nervous energies to seep through your grounding cord. Release this for renewal to Mother Earth. Affirm to yourself: "I am safe in my body in this present moment through my connection to Mother Earth, where I grow stronger within my own personal power." This is your grounding mantra. Let this mantra permeate every fiber of your being, deep into every cell of your body, as you strengthen like a mighty tree towering over a vast forest.

Feel the stability of this grounded state of being as you call upon the archangel Michael to assist you in cutting cords that no longer serve you and hold you back from your power source. Visualize, or ask to be shown, the person or event with whom you need to cut energy cords. Don't overthink or overanalyze it, as you may be surprised with whom or what you have been harboring toxic energy cords. Remember, these are intuitive downloads; we glimpse them in the fraction of a second before our ego starts to analyze what we see.

With your eyes closed, look down again at the glow of

your solar plexus. This is where your freedom through personal power resides. See the energy cords attached to you projecting toward the person or event you are connected with. There are no worries or anxieties about this connection. You are in control through the stability of your grounding to Mother Earth. Surround this person or event in a bubble of white light. You harbor no ill feelings, only wanting the best for all involved. Now, visualize the archangel Michael standing before you. Watch as he swings his mighty sword in a swift and powerful motion upon the cords, severing the connection. Take a deep breath and exhale as you see the cords dissolve. The distance between you and the person or event is growing. Visualize the area where the cords were once connected fully healed and whole again. Say to yourself, "I lovingly send all energy that is not my own back to its sender for healing and transmutation for the highest good of all."

If your intention is to end the energy-cord connection, stop here and give gratitude for the assistance you have received today in clearing unwanted attachments. If you wish to retain a connection with this person or event, reinstate a cord of positive energy between you. It is your choice to reinstate an energy connection on your terms. Visualize a cord filled with pink light and say, "I now allow this cord of light and love to bring about growth and connection for the highest good between us moving forward. So be it, and so it is."

Give thanks to all who assisted you with this practice, and know you are always protected from others' energy cords. You are in control and capable of severing and reconnecting them whenever you choose.

Chapter 15

GRIEF IS LOVE

We never lose our loved ones. They accompany us; they don't disappear from our lives. We are merely in different rooms.

— PAULO COELHO

The grief we feel upon a loved one's death is unbearable, but it can also be one of the most intense versions of love possible because that love is now limitless. In death, we break free of our human shell and transform into pure energy. The body dies, but the energy has always existed and can never be destroyed. That energy exists in a perfect state of love, which is why when someone we love dies, we continue to sense them through our love for them. That love is their eternal soul. In this way, we are inseparable from them because the love itself transcends physical existence.

When we grieve, especially the physical loss of a loved one, there is significant pain, often unlike anything we've ever felt. Some may struggle to breathe, sleep, or eat. Tears may flow for days and at random times. The loss can physically hurt as we wonder how we will continue to live without that person. But the magic begins to happen when we learn to use this raw exposure to love in ways that honor that love. What about that love can inspire us to live differently, live with more love for those around us, and embrace the life we truly want for ourselves? Tragedy has a way of propelling us into new directions because it derails us from our expectations about how things are "supposed to happen," inspiring us to act now so we can live our best life. It is the ultimate case of surrender. We cannot move through it without allowing it to move through us.

Grief is universal and connects us all. Love is the same. When the two collide, such as in death, people usually feel compassion instantly because most can comprehend the magnitude of this pain. We tend to feel an innate reaction to support someone who is suffering, and when someone we love dies, the people we count on for support become critical. We need to be able to be authentic and honest about how we feel with those we trust the most. These people are part of our soul group.

Our soul group comprises our soulmates, and a soulmate is a soul with whom we have lived many lifetimes. They are people with whom we have entered life on a soul level to learn lessons that are meant to help us ascend into a higher state of existence on the other side. This is part of why the grief associated with the physical death of a loved one can be so profound. Part of our soul is here in the living world, while the other part (the person we love) is now on the other side. Our expectation of continuing the journey together feels shattered. While there is some truth to this, it's an illusion. We are never fully separated from our soulmates on the other side. This life is only a blip in the vast orchestra of our soul's journey.

It's a common misconception that a soulmate must be a romantic partner. They can certainly be a spouse or life partner, but these spiritual connections go far beyond romance. A soulmate can be a parent, sibling, child, friend, coworker, neighbor, or anyone else with whom we have a special bond. It can be someone we find at any point in our lives, whether at a young age or in our later years. We can have numerous soulmates throughout our lifetime, and even more than one at the same time.

Sometimes, upon meeting a soulmate, we may instantly be familiar with them. It's also possible that familiarity grows as we get to know them and develop a soul recognition. Regardless of when it happens, this familiarity arises because we get a glimpse of a soul with whom we have spent many lifetimes. It is part of our journey of spiritual evolution.

When you meet someone you believe is a soulmate, you may experience déjà vu. I liken it to when I was sixteen years old and in a horrific car accident. When that happened, I saw my life flash before my eyes. Past experiences, good and bad, were suddenly in front of me. That memory flash is similar to what we feel when we first meet a soulmate. Since we haven't met in this life before, we are not recalling current shared experiences; we are remembering our experiences with them in a previous life, much like an energetic imprint. As we get to know the person and build a relationship with them here on earth, we may continue to have those "flashes" as more of our past experiences with them emerge.

Soulmate relationships are not perfect. They are part of the soul contract set up from the other side before our birth. All souls within a soul group travel together throughout lifetimes to teach each other lessons so the soul can evolve into higher plains of existence. These are roles we play out here in life. We can argue or disagree, but no drama or toxicity can take away the love that exists with a soulmate because it transcends life-times. It stands the test of time — not just our time together here but in previous lives. That is why, even in death, that link cannot be broken.

Grief is a reminder that we have an unbreakable connection with our soulmates. It can change our way of thinking, ideas of self-limitation, and the people we let in going forward. In grief, we also learn the invaluable lesson of letting go. We must let go of the physical relationship with the one we love. But in letting go, we pick up something new. We transform. This transformation, brought on by grief, is an opportunity to forgive. There is no room to hold on to any ill will that separates us from those we love, either those who have crossed over or who are still with us but we have not forgiven. The time for healing ourselves is now.

Grief reminds us that we don't have to hold on to fears, insecurities, or whatever held us back in our youth. That's over now. There is no time for that. We can't go back, only forward. There is no time for negative self-talk because this gets in the way of being happy, expressing who we really are, and living up to our full potential.

Faced with grief, we are reminded of the shortness and fragility of life. We can change the world around us through our actions and words. Losing someone we love reminds us that we only have one opportunity to express our love to those we care most about in this life, so why spend a single moment sending toxic energy to others? If we aren't happy with a relationship, we must cut the negative energy cords now because there is not a moment to lose in living a happy life. We naturally have the tools we need to recognize that we create our world. Our inner world is reflected around us by where we direct our focus. The narrative we create within ourselves about our life will attract more of the same to us.

Life is a challenge and, at times, a struggle. You would not be here if you weren't strong. You are a survivor, and the challenges you face can be your greatest achievements. Embrace those challenges, and don't let any defeat stop you. Don't give up on yourself. Learn to trust your intuition to avoid as many pitfalls as possible along the way. You don't need to wait for earth-shattering grief to start connecting with the other side. Your spiritual web is waiting for you right now to engage them. Start searching for your spiritual path toward that connection. If meditating and reciting mantras accomplish that for you, embrace them; they have worked for me. If you're drawn somewhere else to achieve this connection, I urge you to forge your way there. I hope you enjoy the practices I've shared with you and engage in this relationship you already have with the realm of Spirit.

I dedicated my first book, *Expect the Unexpected*, to my mom with this message: "To my mother Yvonne, who taught me that our light can never be extinguished." This is my same message to you. You are an eternal manifestation of the light of love. May you bring this knowledge into your own life to create your heaven on earth.

Appendix

THE CHAKRAS

C hakras are energy centers located throughout the body.
The **first chakra** is known as the **root chakra** and is
located at the base of the spine. This energy color is dark red.
It represents the element earth and connects us to our survival
instincts and grounds us to our physical self. When this chakra
is aligned properly, it brings us health, prosperity, and security.

The **second chakra** is known as the **sacral chakra** and is
located right below the belly button. This energy color is bright
orange. It represents the element water and connects us to our
emotions, sexuality, and sensuality. Remember that sensuality
involves the senses — the feelings that rush through us when
we see, hear, or smell something. When aligned properly, this
chakra brings us gracefulness and fluidity, allows us to feel
deeply, enables us to have our sexual desires fulfilled, and allows change and acceptance in our lives.

The **third chakra** is known as the **solar plexus chakra** and
is located right below the sternum and diaphragm. This energy color is yellow. This chakra brings us a feeling of personal
power, as if we can rule the world!

The **fourth chakra** is known as the **heart chakra** and is
located in the middle of our chest next to our heart. This energy color is green. It represents love and understanding of

humankind. When aligned properly, this chakra allows us to love unconditionally and feel a deep sense of compassion for others and the world.

The **fifth chakra** is known as the **throat chakra** and is located in the throat above the larynx. This energy color is dark blue. It represents communication and passion for creativity. When aligned properly, this chakra allows us to speak our truth in all matters and communicate openly and freely.

The **sixth chakra** is known as the **third-eye chakra** and is located on the forehead, between the brows, in the third-eye center. This energy color is indigo. It represents clear vision. When aligned properly, this chakra allows us to see information psychically, as well as see the reality of a situation.

The **seventh chakra** is known as the **crown chakra** and is located at the top of the head. Its energy color is purple, or purple with a halo of crystal white. It represents awareness. When aligned properly, we feel connected to oneness, the Creator of all that is, and feel a state of bliss.

ACKNOWLEDGMENTS

I would first like to thank my phenomenal publisher, New World Library, for their continued support and for giving me an opportunity to get my message out to readers — that we all have our eternal connection with the other side.

I want to give special thanks to my editor Georgia Hughes for all your love and guidance over the years, and for believing in me. And I must give thanks to Jeff Campbell, my copyeditor, who has a gift for taking the written word and polishing it with such beautiful honesty and clarity.

As always, I must thank my mother Yvonne, in spirit, for being my guiding light in this life, and for bringing the realm of Spirit to all of us.

I want to give a big thank-you to my coauthor William Croyle for all your hard work, support, dedication to understanding my process, and continued friendship over the years. What a wonderful journey it has been.

I must thank my partner, Patrick Markert, for your unconditional love and support, for your ability to mold my thoughts and ideas into written words, and for helping me find my voice. I could not have done this without you.

Thank you to Michelle Larson for your beautiful friendship

and your love, and for allowing me to share your inspiring story with others.

I want to thank my dear friend Brittany Hicks, my earth angel in this life, who inspired me so many years ago to look at life from a new perspective, and who continues to uplift and inspire me today. You are a bright light in this world.

I would like to thank my friends and family — my earth-bound soul group — for their unwavering support over the years.

I cannot thank all my clients enough. It is your continued support, love, and appreciation that continue to motivate me to keep spreading my message from Spirit. Thank you, thank you, thank you.

I could not forget to thank the ones who have loved me without conditions — my dear doggies, Teddy, Balto, and Sam, who were at my feet every day during the writing of this book. Their love and companionship are unsurpassed.

Finally, I must thank Spirit for your unwavering love, guidance, and trust in me, so I may be of service to others.

ABOUT BILL PHILIPPS

Bill Philipps is a psychic medium and spiritual teacher who helps the deceased communicate with their loved ones on earth. Bill's fresh, upbeat, and direct approach perfectly complements his warm and relatable demeanor, captivating audiences worldwide.

Bill studied music at the San Francisco Conservatory of Music, where he graduated in 2008 with a degree in vocal performance. He found that music, in a deeply spiritual way, enabled him to tune in to and further develop his psychic medium abilities, which date to his early childhood.

Bill's guidance is sought by many who seek answers about life and the afterlife, including top executives, celebrities, and everyday people. He has appeared on the *Dr. Phil* show, *Access Hollywood*, and various other television and radio broadcasts. He conducts individual readings in person and virtually. He also offers small-group and audience readings throughout the United States. He lives in Southern California with his partner and three dogs. You can learn more about Bill at BillPhilipps.com.

ABOUT WILLIAM CROYLE

Coauthor William Croyle is a native of Cleveland, Ohio, and a graduate of St. Ignatius High School and Ashland University. He is the author of eleven other books with some of the world's most inspirational people. He lives in Erlanger, Kentucky, with his wife, Debra, and their three sons. More information on his books is available at WilliamCroyle.com and at Facebook.com/WilliamCroyleBooks.